STAAR

Grade 8 Reading Assessment

SECRETS

Study Guide
Your Key to Exam Success

STAAR Test Review for the
State of Texas Assessments
of Academic Readiness

Dear Future Exam Success Story:

First of all, **THANK YOU** for purchasing Mometrix study materials!

Second, congratulations! You are one of the few determined test-takers who are committed to doing whatever it takes to excel on your exam. **You have come to the right place.** We developed these study materials with one goal in mind: to deliver you the information you need in a format that's concise and easy to use.

In addition to optimizing your guide for the content of the test, we've outlined our recommended steps for breaking down the preparation process into small, attainable goals so you can make sure you stay on track.

We've also analyzed the entire test-taking process, identifying the most common pitfalls and showing how you can overcome them and be ready for any curveball the test throws you.

Standardized testing is one of the biggest obstacles on your road to success, which only increases the importance of doing well in the high-pressure, high-stakes environment of test day. Your results on this test could have a significant impact on your future, and this guide provides the information and practical advice to help you achieve your full potential on test day.

Your success is our success

We would love to hear from you! If you would like to share the story of your exam success or if you have any questions or comments in regard to our products, please contact us at **800-673-8175** or **support@mometrix.com**.

Thanks again for your business and we wish you continued success!

Sincerely,
The Mometrix Test Preparation Team

Need more help? Check out our flashcards at: http://MometrixFlashcards.com/STAAR

TABLE OF CONTENTS

INTRODUCTION 1

SECRET KEY #1 – PLAN BIG, STUDY SMALL 2
INFORMATION ORGANIZATION 2
TIME MANAGEMENT 2
STUDY ENVIRONMENT 2

SECRET KEY #2 – MAKE YOUR STUDYING COUNT 3
RETENTION 3
MODALITY 3

SECRET KEY #3 – PRACTICE THE RIGHT WAY 4
PRACTICE TEST STRATEGY 5

SECRET KEY #4 – PACE YOURSELF 6

SECRET KEY #5 – HAVE A PLAN FOR GUESSING 7
WHEN TO START THE GUESSING PROCESS 7
HOW TO NARROW DOWN THE CHOICES 8
WHICH ANSWER TO CHOOSE 9

TEST-TAKING STRATEGIES 10
QUESTION STRATEGIES 10
ANSWER CHOICE STRATEGIES 11
GENERAL STRATEGIES 12
FINAL NOTES 13

READING ASSESSMENT 15

READING PRACTICE TEST #1 29

ANSWER KEY AND EXPLANATIONS FOR READING TEST #1 45

READING PRACTICE TEST #2 55

ANSWER KEY AND EXPLANATIONS FOR READING TEST #2 70

HOW TO OVERCOME TEST ANXIETY 80
CAUSES OF TEST ANXIETY 80
ELEMENTS OF TEST ANXIETY 81
EFFECTS OF TEST ANXIETY 81
PHYSICAL STEPS FOR BEATING TEST ANXIETY 82
MENTAL STEPS FOR BEATING TEST ANXIETY 83
STUDY STRATEGY 84
TEST TIPS 86
IMPORTANT QUALIFICATION 87

THANK YOU 88

ADDITIONAL BONUS MATERIAL 89

Introduction

Thank you for purchasing this resource! You have made the choice to prepare yourself for a test that could have a huge impact on your future, and this guide is designed to help you be fully ready for test day. Obviously, it's important to have a solid understanding of the test material, but you also need to be prepared for the unique environment and stressors of the test, so that you can perform to the best of your abilities.

For this purpose, the first section that appears in this guide is the **Secret Keys**. We've devoted countless hours to meticulously researching what works and what doesn't, and we've boiled down our findings to the five most impactful steps you can take to improve your performance on the test. We start at the beginning with study planning and move through the preparation process, all the way to the testing strategies that will help you get the most out of what you know when you're finally sitting in front of the test.

We recommend that you start preparing for your test as far in advance as possible. However, if you've bought this guide as a last-minute study resource and only have a few days before your test, we recommend that you skip over the first two Secret Keys since they address a long-term study plan.

If you struggle with **test anxiety**, we strongly encourage you to check out our recommendations for how you can overcome it. Test anxiety is a formidable foe, but it can be beaten, and we want to make sure you have the tools you need to defeat it.

Secret Key #1 – Plan Big, Study Small

There's a lot riding on your performance. If you want to ace this test, you're going to need to keep your skills sharp and the material fresh in your mind. You need a plan that lets you review everything you need to know while still fitting in your schedule. We'll break this strategy down into three categories.

Information Organization

Start with the information you already have: the official test outline. From this, you can make a complete list of all the concepts you need to cover before the test. Organize these concepts into groups that can be studied together, and create a list of any related vocabulary you need to learn so you can brush up on any difficult terms. You'll want to keep this vocabulary list handy once you actually start studying since you may need to add to it along the way.

Time Management

Once you have your set of study concepts, decide how to spread them out over the time you have left before the test. Break your study plan into small, clear goals so you have a manageable task for each day and know exactly what you're doing. Then just focus on one small step at a time. When you manage your time this way, you don't need to spend hours at a time studying. Studying a small block of content for a short period each day helps you retain information better and avoid stressing over how much you have left to do. You can relax knowing that you have a plan to cover everything in time. In order for this strategy to be effective though, you have to start studying early and stick to your schedule. Avoid the exhaustion and futility that comes from last-minute cramming!

Study Environment

The environment you study in has a big impact on your learning. Studying in a coffee shop, while probably more enjoyable, is not likely to be as fruitful as studying in a quiet room. It's important to keep distractions to a minimum. You're only planning to study for a short block of time, so make the most of it. Don't pause to check your phone or get up to find a snack. It's also important to **avoid multitasking**. Research has consistently shown that multitasking will make your studying dramatically less effective. Your study area should also be comfortable and well-lit so you don't have the distraction of straining your eyes or sitting on an uncomfortable chair.

The time of day you study is also important. You want to be rested and alert. Don't wait until just before bedtime. Study when you'll be most likely to comprehend and remember. Even better, if you know what time of day your test will be, set that time aside for study. That way your brain will be used to working on that subject at that specific time and you'll have a better chance of recalling information.

Finally, it can be helpful to team up with others who are studying for the same test. Your actual studying should be done in as isolated an environment as possible, but the work of organizing the information and setting up the study plan can be divided up. In between study sessions, you can discuss with your teammates the concepts that you're all studying and quiz each other on the details. Just be sure that your teammates are as serious about the test as you are. If you find that your study time is being replaced with social time, you might need to find a new team.

Secret Key #2 – Make Your Studying Count

You're devoting a lot of time and effort to preparing for this test, so you want to be absolutely certain it will pay off. This means doing more than just reading the content and hoping you can remember it on test day. It's important to make every minute of study count. There are two main areas you can focus on to make your studying count:

Retention

It doesn't matter how much time you study if you can't remember the material. You need to make sure you are retaining the concepts. To check your retention of the information you're learning, try recalling it at later times with minimal prompting. Try carrying around flashcards and glance at one or two from time to time or ask a friend who's also studying for the test to quiz you.

To enhance your retention, look for ways to put the information into practice so that you can apply it rather than simply recalling it. If you're using the information in practical ways, it will be much easier to remember. Similarly, it helps to solidify a concept in your mind if you're not only reading it to yourself but also explaining it to someone else. Ask a friend to let you teach them about a concept you're a little shaky on (or speak aloud to an imaginary audience if necessary). As you try to summarize, define, give examples, and answer your friend's questions, you'll understand the concepts better and they will stay with you longer. Finally, step back for a big picture view and ask yourself how each piece of information fits with the whole subject. When you link the different concepts together and see them working together as a whole, it's easier to remember the individual components.

Finally, practice showing your work on any multi-step problems, even if you're just studying. Writing out each step you take to solve a problem will help solidify the process in your mind, and you'll be more likely to remember it during the test.

Modality

Modality simply refers to the means or method by which you study. Choosing a study modality that fits your own individual learning style is crucial. No two people learn best in exactly the same way, so it's important to know your strengths and use them to your advantage.

For example, if you learn best by visualization, focus on visualizing a concept in your mind and draw an image or a diagram. Try color-coding your notes, illustrating them, or creating symbols that will trigger your mind to recall a learned concept. If you learn best by hearing or discussing information, find a study partner who learns the same way or read aloud to yourself. Think about how to put the information in your own words. Imagine that you are giving a lecture on the topic and record yourself so you can listen to it later.

For any learning style, flashcards can be helpful. Organize the information so you can take advantage of spare moments to review. Underline key words or phrases. Use different colors for different categories. Mnemonic devices (such as creating a short list in which every item starts with the same letter) can also help with retention. Find what works best for you and use it to store the information in your mind most effectively and easily.

Secret Key #3 – Practice the Right Way

Your success on test day depends not only on how many hours you put into preparing, but also on whether you prepared the right way. It's good to check along the way to see if your studying is paying off. One of the most effective ways to do this is by taking practice tests to evaluate your progress. Practice tests are useful because they show exactly where you need to improve. Every time you take a practice test, pay special attention to these three groups of questions:

- The questions you got wrong
- The questions you had to guess on, even if you guessed right
- The questions you found difficult or slow to work through

This will show you exactly what your weak areas are, and where you need to devote more study time. Ask yourself why each of these questions gave you trouble. Was it because you didn't understand the material? Was it because you didn't remember the vocabulary? Do you need more repetitions on this type of question to build speed and confidence? Dig into those questions and figure out how you can strengthen your weak areas as you go back to review the material.

Additionally, many practice tests have a section explaining the answer choices. It can be tempting to read the explanation and think that you now have a good understanding of the concept. However, an explanation likely only covers part of the question's broader context. Even if the explanation makes sense, **go back and investigate** every concept related to the question until you're positive you have a thorough understanding.

As you go along, keep in mind that the practice test is just that: practice. Memorizing these questions and answers will not be very helpful on the actual test because it is unlikely to have any of the same exact questions. If you only know the right answers to the sample questions, you won't be prepared for the real thing. **Study the concepts** until you understand them fully, and then you'll be able to answer any question that shows up on the test.

It's important to wait on the practice tests until you're ready. If you take a test on your first day of study, you may be overwhelmed by the amount of material covered and how much you need to learn. Work up to it gradually.

On test day, you'll need to be prepared for answering questions, managing your time, and using the test-taking strategies you've learned. It's a lot to balance, like a mental marathon that will have a big impact on your future. Like training for a marathon, you'll need to start slowly and work your way up. When test day arrives, you'll be ready.

Start with the strategies you've read in the first two Secret Keys—plan your course and study in the way that works best for you. If you have time, consider using multiple study resources to get different approaches to the same concepts. It can be helpful to see difficult concepts from more than one angle. Then find a good source for practice tests. Many times, the test website will suggest potential study resources or provide sample tests.

Practice Test Strategy

When you're ready to start taking practice tests, follow this strategy:

Untimed and Open-Book Practice

Take the first test with no time constraints and with your notes and study guide handy. Take your time and focus on applying the strategies you've learned.

Timed and Open-Book Practice

Take the second practice test open-book as well, but set a timer and practice pacing yourself to finish in time.

Timed and Closed-Book Practice

Take any other practice tests as if it were test day. Set a timer and put away your study materials. Sit at a table or desk in a quiet room, imagine yourself at the testing center, and answer questions as quickly and accurately as possible.

Keep repeating timed and closed-book tests on a regular basis until you run out of practice tests or it's time for the actual test. Your mind will be ready for the schedule and stress of test day, and you'll be able to focus on recalling the material you've learned.

Secret Key #4 – Pace Yourself

Once you're fully prepared for the material on the test, your biggest challenge on test day will be managing your time. Just knowing that the clock is ticking can make you panic even if you have plenty of time left. Work on pacing yourself so you can build confidence against the time constraints of the exam. Pacing is a difficult skill to master, especially in a high-pressure environment, so **practice is vital**.

Set time expectations for your pace based on how much time is available. For example, if a section has 60 questions and the time limit is 30 minutes, you know you have to average 30 seconds or less per question in order to answer them all. Although 30 seconds is the hard limit, set 25 seconds per question as your goal, so you reserve extra time to spend on harder questions. When you budget extra time for the harder questions, you no longer have any reason to stress when those questions take longer to answer.

Don't let this time expectation distract you from working through the test at a calm, steady pace, but keep it in mind so you don't spend too much time on any one question. Recognize that taking extra time on one question you don't understand may keep you from answering two that you do understand later in the test. If your time limit for a question is up and you're still not sure of the answer, mark it and move on, and come back to it later if the time and the test format allow. If the testing format doesn't allow you to return to earlier questions, just make an educated guess; then put it out of your mind and move on.

On the easier questions, be careful not to rush. It may seem wise to hurry through them so you have more time for the challenging ones, but it's not worth missing one if you know the concept and just didn't take the time to read the question fully. Work efficiently but make sure you understand the question and have looked at all of the answer choices, since more than one may seem right at first.

Even if you're paying attention to the time, you may find yourself a little behind at some point. You should speed up to get back on track, but do so wisely. Don't panic; just take a few seconds less on each question until you're caught up. Don't guess without thinking, but do look through the answer choices and eliminate any you know are wrong. If you can get down to two choices, it is often worthwhile to guess from those. Once you've chosen an answer, move on and don't dwell on any that you skipped or had to hurry through. If a question was taking too long, chances are it was one of the harder ones, so you weren't as likely to get it right anyway.

On the other hand, if you find yourself getting ahead of schedule, it may be beneficial to slow down a little. The more quickly you work, the more likely you are to make a careless mistake that will affect your score. You've budgeted time for each question, so don't be afraid to spend that time. Practice an efficient but careful pace to get the most out of the time you have.

Secret Key #5 – Have a Plan for Guessing

When you're taking the test, you may find yourself stuck on a question. Some of the answer choices seem better than others, but you don't see the one answer choice that is obviously correct. What do you do?

The scenario described above is very common, yet most test takers have not effectively prepared for it. Developing and practicing a plan for guessing may be one of the single most effective uses of your time as you get ready for the exam.

In developing your plan for guessing, there are three questions to address:

- When should you start the guessing process?
- How should you narrow down the choices?
- Which answer should you choose?

When to Start the Guessing Process

Unless your plan for guessing is to select C every time (which, despite its merits, is not what we recommend), you need to leave yourself enough time to apply your answer elimination strategies. Since you have a limited amount of time for each question, that means that if you're going to give yourself the best shot at guessing correctly, you have to decide quickly whether or not you will guess.

Of course, the best-case scenario is that you don't have to guess at all, so first, see if you can answer the question based on your knowledge of the subject and basic reasoning skills. Focus on the key words in the question and try to jog your memory of related topics. Give yourself a chance to bring the knowledge to mind, but once you realize that you don't have (or you can't access) the knowledge you need to answer the question, it's time to start the guessing process.

It's almost always better to start the guessing process too early than too late. It only takes a few seconds to remember something and answer the question from knowledge. Carefully eliminating wrong answer choices takes longer. Plus, going through the process of eliminating answer choices can actually help jog your memory.

Summary: Start the guessing process as soon as you decide that you can't answer the question based on your knowledge.

How to Narrow Down the Choices

The next chapter in this book (**Test-Taking Strategies**) includes a wide range of strategies for how to approach questions and how to look for answer choices to eliminate. You will definitely want to read those carefully, practice them, and figure out which ones work best for you. Here though, we're going to address a mindset rather than a particular strategy.

Your chances of guessing an answer correctly depend on how many options you are choosing from.

How many choices you have	How likely you are to guess correctly
5	20%
4	25%
3	33%
2	50%
1	100%

You can see from this chart just how valuable it is to be able to eliminate incorrect answers and make an educated guess, but there are two things that many test takers do that cause them to miss out on the benefits of guessing:

- Accidentally eliminating the correct answer
- Selecting an answer based on an impression

We'll look at the first one here, and the second one in the next section.

To avoid accidentally eliminating the correct answer, we recommend a thought exercise called **the $5 challenge**. In this challenge, you only eliminate an answer choice from contention if you are willing to bet $5 on it being wrong. Why $5? Five dollars is a small but not insignificant amount of money. It's an amount you could afford to lose but wouldn't want to throw away. And while losing $5 once might not hurt too much, doing it twenty times will set you back $100. In the same way, each small decision you make—eliminating a choice here, guessing on a question there—won't by itself impact your score very much, but when you put them all together, they can make a big difference. By holding each answer choice elimination decision to a higher standard, you can reduce the risk of accidentally eliminating the correct answer.

The $5 challenge can also be applied in a positive sense: If you are willing to bet $5 that an answer choice *is* correct, go ahead and mark it as correct.

Summary: Only eliminate an answer choice if you are willing to bet $5 that it is wrong.

Which Answer to Choose

You're taking the test. You've run into a hard question and decided you'll have to guess. You've eliminated all the answer choices you're willing to bet $5 on. Now you have to pick an answer. Why do we even need to talk about this? Why can't you just pick whichever one you feel like when the time comes?

The answer to these questions is that if you don't come into the test with a plan, you'll rely on your impression to select an answer choice, and if you do that, you risk falling into a trap. The test writers know that everyone who takes their test will be guessing on some of the questions, so they intentionally write wrong answer choices to seem plausible. You still have to pick an answer though, and if the wrong answer choices are designed to look right, how can you ever be sure that you're not falling for their trap? The best solution we've found to this dilemma is to take the decision out of your hands entirely. Here is the process we recommend:

Once you've eliminated any choices that you are confident (willing to bet $5) are wrong, select the first remaining choice as your answer.

Whether you choose to select the first remaining choice, the second, or the last, the important thing is that you use some preselected standard. Using this approach guarantees that you will not be enticed into selecting an answer choice that looks right, because you are not basing your decision on how the answer choices look.

This is not meant to make you question your knowledge. Instead, it is to help you recognize the difference between your knowledge and your impressions. There's a huge difference between thinking an answer is right because of what you know, and thinking an answer is right because it looks or sounds like it should be right.

Summary: To ensure that your selection is appropriately random, make a predetermined selection from among all answer choices you have not eliminated.

Test-Taking Strategies

This section contains a list of test-taking strategies that you may find helpful as you work through the test. By taking what you know and applying logical thought, you can maximize your chances of answering any question correctly!

It is very important to realize that every question is different and every person is different: no single strategy will work on every question, and no single strategy will work for every person. That's why we've included all of them here, so you can try them out and determine which ones work best for different types of questions and which ones work best for you.

Question Strategies

Read Carefully

Read the question and answer choices carefully. Don't miss the question because you misread the terms. You have plenty of time to read each question thoroughly and make sure you understand what is being asked. Yet a happy medium must be attained, so don't waste too much time. You must read carefully, but efficiently.

Contextual Clues

Look for contextual clues. If the question includes a word you are not familiar with, look at the immediate context for some indication of what the word might mean. Contextual clues can often give you all the information you need to decipher the meaning of an unfamiliar word. Even if you can't determine the meaning, you may be able to narrow down the possibilities enough to make a solid guess at the answer to the question.

Prefixes

If you're having trouble with a word in the question or answer choices, try dissecting it. Take advantage of every clue that the word might include. Prefixes and suffixes can be a huge help. Usually they allow you to determine a basic meaning. Pre- means before, post- means after, pro - is positive, de- is negative. From prefixes and suffixes, you can get an idea of the general meaning of the word and try to put it into context.

Hedge Words

Watch out for critical hedge words, such as *likely, may, can, sometimes, often, almost, mostly, usually, generally, rarely,* and *sometimes.* Question writers insert these hedge phrases to cover every possibility. Often an answer choice will be wrong simply because it leaves no room for exception. Be on guard for answer choices that have definitive words such as *exactly* and *always.*

Switchback Words

Stay alert for *switchbacks.* These are the words and phrases frequently used to alert you to shifts in thought. The most common switchback words are *but, although,* and *however.* Others include *nevertheless, on the other hand, even though, while, in spite of, despite, regardless of.* Switchback words are important to catch because they can change the direction of the question or an answer choice.

Face Value

When in doubt, use common sense. Accept the situation in the problem at face value. Don't read too much into it. These problems will not require you to make wild assumptions. If you have to go beyond creativity and warp time or space in order to have an answer choice fit the question, then you should move on and consider the other answer choices. These are normal problems rooted in reality. The applicable relationship or explanation may not be readily apparent, but it is there for you to figure out. Use your common sense to interpret anything that isn't clear.

Answer Choice Strategies

Answer Selection

The most thorough way to pick an answer choice is to identify and eliminate wrong answers until only one is left, then confirm it is the correct answer. Sometimes an answer choice may immediately seem right, but be careful. The test writers will usually put more than one reasonable answer choice on each question, so take a second to read all of them and make sure that the other choices are not equally obvious. As long as you have time left, it is better to read every answer choice than to pick the first one that looks right without checking the others.

Answer Choice Families

An answer choice family consists of two (in rare cases, three) answer choices that are very similar in construction and cannot all be true at the same time. If you see two answer choices that are direct opposites or parallels, one of them is usually the correct answer. For instance, if one answer choice says that quantity x increases and another either says that quantity x decreases (opposite) or says that quantity y increases (parallel), then those answer choices would fall into the same family. An answer choice that doesn't match the construction of the answer choice family is more likely to be incorrect. Most questions will not have answer choice families, but when they do appear, you should be prepared to recognize them.

Eliminate Answers

Eliminate answer choices as soon as you realize they are wrong, but make sure you consider all possibilities. If you are eliminating answer choices and realize that the last one you are left with is also wrong, don't panic. Start over and consider each choice again. There may be something you missed the first time that you will realize on the second pass.

Avoid Fact Traps

Don't be distracted by an answer choice that is factually true but doesn't answer the question. You are looking for the choice that answers the question. Stay focused on what the question is asking for so you don't accidentally pick an answer that is true but incorrect. Always go back to the question and make sure the answer choice you've selected actually answers the question and is not merely a true statement.

Extreme Statements

In general, you should avoid answers that put forth extreme actions as standard practice or proclaim controversial ideas as established fact. An answer choice that states the "process should be used in certain situations, if..." is much more likely to be correct than one that states the "process should be discontinued completely." The first is a calm rational statement and doesn't even make a definitive, uncompromising stance, using a hedge word *if* to provide wiggle room, whereas the second choice is a radical idea and far more extreme.

Benchmark

As you read through the answer choices and you come across one that seems to answer the question well, mentally select that answer choice. This is not your final answer, but it's the one that will help you evaluate the other answer choices. The one that you selected is your benchmark or standard for judging each of the other answer choices. Every other answer choice must be compared to your benchmark. That choice is correct until proven otherwise by another answer choice beating it. If you find a better answer, then that one becomes your new benchmark. Once you've decided that no other choice answers the question as well as your benchmark, you have your final answer.

Predict the Answer

Before you even start looking at the answer choices, it is often best to try to predict the answer. When you come up with the answer on your own, it is easier to avoid distractions and traps because you will know exactly what to look for. The right answer choice is unlikely to be word-for-word what you came up with, but it should be a close match. Even if you are confident that you have the right answer, you should still take the time to read each option before moving on.

General Strategies

Tough Questions

If you are stumped on a problem or it appears too hard or too difficult, don't waste time. Move on! Remember though, if you can quickly check for obviously incorrect answer choices, your chances of guessing correctly are greatly improved. Before you completely give up, at least try to knock out a couple of possible answers. Eliminate what you can and then guess at the remaining answer choices before moving on.

Check Your Work

Since you will probably not know every term listed and the answer to every question, it is important that you get credit for the ones that you do know. Don't miss any questions through careless mistakes. If at all possible, try to take a second to look back over your answer selection and make sure you've selected the correct answer choice and haven't made a costly careless mistake (such as marking an answer choice that you didn't mean to mark). This quick double check should more than pay for itself in caught mistakes for the time it costs.

Pace Yourself

It's easy to be overwhelmed when you're looking at a page full of questions; your mind is confused and full of random thoughts, and the clock is ticking down faster than you would like. Calm down and maintain the pace that you have set for yourself. Especially as you get down to the last few minutes of the test, don't let the small numbers on the clock make you panic. As long as you are on track by monitoring your pace, you are guaranteed to have time for each question.

Don't Rush

It is very easy to make errors when you are in a hurry. Maintaining a fast pace in answering questions is pointless if it makes you miss questions that you would have gotten right otherwise. Test writers like to include distracting information and wrong answers that seem right. Taking a little extra time to avoid careless mistakes can make all the difference in your test score. Find a pace that allows you to be confident in the answers that you select.

Keep Moving

Panicking will not help you pass the test, so do your best to stay calm and keep moving. Taking deep breaths and going through the answer elimination steps you practiced can help to break through a stress barrier and keep your pace.

Final Notes

The combination of a solid foundation of content knowledge and the confidence that comes from practicing your plan for applying that knowledge is the key to maximizing your performance on test day. As your foundation of content knowledge is built up and strengthened, you'll find that the strategies included in this chapter become more and more effective in helping you quickly sift through the distractions and traps of the test to isolate the correct answer.

Now it's time to move on to the test content chapters of this book, but be sure to keep your goal in mind. As you read, think about how you will be able to apply this information on the test. If you've already seen sample questions for the test and you have an idea of the question format and style, try to come up with questions of your own that you can answer based on what you're reading. This will give you valuable practice applying your knowledge in the same ways you can expect to on test day.

Good luck and good studying!

Reading Assessment

Prefix, suffix, and root word

Root word: The base part of a compound word when one takes away any prefixes or suffixes. The root carries the base meaning that the prefix or suffix alters.

Prefix: A part of a word that is added onto the front of a root word and cannot stand alone. It does have its own meaning, so it changes or enhances the meaning of the root word to make a new word. For example, the prefix *un-* changes the meaning of the root *happy* when it is added: *un*happy means *not* happy.

Suffix: A part of a word that is added onto the end of a root word and, like a prefix, cannot stand alone. It also has its own meaning so it changes or enhances the meaning of the root word to make a new word. For example, the suffix *-ness* changes the meaning of the root *happy*: happi*ness* means *the state of* being happy.

Knowledge of prefixes and suffixes can help one determine the meaning of an unfamiliar word by helping to break the word down into all of its parts: prefix + root word + suffix. Look first at the individual meanings of the root word, prefix and/or suffix. Using knowledge of the meaning(s) of the prefix and/or suffix to see what information it adds to the root. Even if the meaning of the root is unknown, one can use knowledge of the prefix's and/or suffix's meaning(s) to determine an approximate meaning of the word. For example, if one sees the word *uninspired* and does not know what it means, they can use the knowledge that *un-* means 'not' to know that the full word means "not inspired."

Examples

The word orthography can be broken down into the following parts: ortho + graph + y. The prefix of the word is ortho-, meaning 'straight' or 'correct'. The root of the word is graph, which means 'write', 'draw', or 'written'. The suffix of the word is -y, which changes the word to a noun when added to the end of it, and means 'state' or 'condition'. Using this knowledge, an approximate definition of the word orthography would be "the state of being written correctly." The dictionary definition of the word orthography is "writing words using the proper letters." The approximate definition taken from the parts can often be close to the true definition.

The word *geometric* can be broken down into the following parts: geo + metri + ic. The prefix of the word is *geo-,* meaning 'earth'. The root of the word is *metri-* (similar in meaning to the root *meter-*), which means 'measure'. The suffix of the word is *-ic,* meaning 'having to do with'. Using this knowledge, an approximate definition of the word *geometric* would be "having to do with measuring the earth." The dictionary definition of the word *geometric* is "of or relating to the branch of mathematics that has to do with measuring points, lines, and angles."

Common prefixes

The following is a list of commonly used prefixes:

- *anti-* : opposite. Example word: antiwar.
- *auto-*: self. Example word: autograph.
- *bi-*: two. Example word: bicycle.
- *bio-*: life, living. Example word: biology.
- *circum-*: around. Example word: circumference.

- *con-, com-*: with, together. Example words: construct, combine.
- *de-*: from, down, away. Example word: derail.
- *dis-*: not, negative. Example word: disregard.
- *in-, im-*: not. Example words: inequality, impossible.
- *inter-*: between. Example word: international.
- *mis-*: bad, badly. Example word: misunderstand.
- *non-*: not. Example word: nonsense.
- *re-*: back, again. Example word: react.
- *sub-*: under, below. Example word: submarine.
- *un-*: not. Example word: unhappy.

Common suffixes

The following is a list of commonly used suffixes:

- *-able, -ible*: capable of. Example words: available, invisible.
- *-ance, -ence*: quality or process. Example words: resistance, independence.
- *-er, -or*: person who. Example words: writer, contactor.
- *-ful*: full of. Example word: thoughtful.
- *-ion, -tion*: condition or action. Example words: narration, evolution.
- *-ism*: belief. Example word: socialism.
- *-ist*: person or member. Example word: internist.
- *-ment*: condition. Example word: enjoyment.
- *-nes* : state or condition. Example word: emptiness.
- *-ship*: state of being connected. Example word: relationship.
- *-y*: state or condition. Example word: windy.

Context clues

Context clues are hints about the meaning of a word. They are the words or phrases in the sentence or sentences before and after a new word. Context clues give the reader an idea about what a word means. These words and phrases may contain a synonym of the new word. (A synonym means the same thing as the word.) These words and phrases may contain an antonym of the new word. (An antonym means the opposite of the word.) A context clue may also contain words that help define the new word or an example of what the new word means. By using context clues, the reader can figure out the meaning of a new word.

Words with multiple meanings

Some words are spelled exactly the same but have different meanings in different contexts. One needs to use the context of the situation to determine the correct meaning of the word in each case. Often, these words can be used as either a noun or a verb and their grammatical usage determines the meaning. The word *trip*, for example, could be either a noun or a verb. *Trip* as a noun means 'vacation', where *trip* as a verb means to fall over something. Here are two different sentences using *trip* as a noun and a verb.

1. Last year, she went on an amazing *trip* to Santa Fe, New Mexico, with her sister.
2. If you aren't watching where you are going, you might *trip* over a bump in the cement.

The word *degree* has at least three different meanings, depending on the situation in which the word is used: (a) a *degree* is the incremental measurement of temperature; (b) a *degree* is a title awarded upon graduation from college; and (c) *degree* can mean the extent or amount of something. Here are three different sentences, each using one of these meanings of the word *degree*:

1. You probably don't notice a difference when the temperature rises one *degree*.
2. The employer is only willing to hire someone with a *degree* in mathematics.
3. It was hard to tell the *degree* to which he really cared about the outcome.

Dictionary, glossary, and thesaurus

One tool that can be used to build word meanings is the dictionary. A dictionary contains words listed alphabetically. It tells each word's meaning. It also tells the word's part of speech. Dictionaries can be books or be online. Glossaries are like dictionaries, but they are smaller than dictionaries. Glossaries list words alphabetically. They tell each word's meaning. They are found at the back of books, and they list words in the books. A thesaurus is a tool that has synonyms of words. For example, if you look up the word happy in a thesaurus, you would see the words content, pleased, glad, joyful, and delighted. A thesaurus does not give a definition like a dictionary does, but you can use a thesaurus to help figure out the meaning of an unfamiliar word. If you are familiar with some of the synonyms of the word, you can determine a precise meaning of the unfamiliar word. For example, if you looked up the word exultant and saw the synonyms overjoyed and thrilled, this could lead you to its meaning "extremely happy."

Mythologies from different cultures

Each culture has its own views about the afterlife, and the roles of their deities, but there are occasional similarities. Some of the most popular figures in mythology are the Greek gods. The Greeks have a multitude of gods, each of which controls a different aspect of life. For example, Hades is the god of the underworld, Poseidon is god of the sea, Athena is goddess of wisdom, and Zeus is king of the gods. In Greek mythology after death your soul would go to the underworld where it would be judged, and you would spend eternity in one of four places based on that judgment. In contrast, Chinese mythology generally had just one deity, but concept of this deity changed over time. Around 200 A.D. it was known as Pangu. Over the years, the name has been Nuwa, Tian, YuDi, and Shangdi. In Chinese mythology, there are many souls, or many parts to the soul, and when someone dies, each part will go somewhere different. For instance, the po is said to remain with the body, while the hun would reside in the family's ancestor tablets.

Denotation and connotation

Denotation is the literal meaning, or dictionary definition, of a word and is a completely objective meaning. Connotation is the meaning of a word as it is derived from the literal meaning <u>plus</u> the emotions or thoughts that one has about the word based on experiences, memories, feelings, and ideas. The connotation of a word is subjective, depending upon the thoughts and feelings of the reader and the situation in which the word is used. The words 'cheap' and 'inexpensive' both have the same denotative meaning of "not costing a lot of money." The word 'cheap', however, has the connotation of being "of low quality" whereas the word 'inexpensive' does not have that. Another example is the word *rat*. The denotative meaning of the word *rat* is a long-tailed rodent. Many people have strong emotions associated with rats so the connotative meaning may include views such as dirty, sleazy, and disgusting. Using the connotative meaning, one could call a sleazy person a rat even though he or she is not a long-tailed rodent.

Here are two different sentences using the denotative and connotative meaning of the word *snake*:

1. One of the largest types of snake is the boa constrictor.
2. If he weren't such a snake, we could rely on him to tell the truth.

The word *snake* has both a denotative and connotative meaning. In the first sentence, the word *snake* is used literally, as a reptile without legs. In the second sentence, the word *snake* is not used to refer to a reptile, but rather a person. This is how one knows that the connotative meaning of the word is being used. One can then use the context of the sentence to determine the connotative meaning of the word: in this case, a crafty, unreliable person.

Universal themes in literature

The theme of a piece of literature is its controlling idea. Universal themes are themes that can be discussed in regard to all of humanity. People all over the world can relate to stories that center on the struggle of man versus man, for example. Other universal themes include man versus nature, man versus himself, good versus evil, fate versus free will, triumph over adversity, and coming of age. Determine the theme of the following short paragraph:

Matt had spent a lot of time preparing for his first babysitting experience. Matt stayed fully attentive to his young cousin, Toby, while he played outside. When his aunt returned, Matt was proud to report that all had gone well. He had acted in the adult role.

The theme of a piece of literature is its controlling idea. The short paragraph shown here is a coming of age story. This means that the protagonist goes through some kind of experience that changes him or her from a child into an adult. By preparing to care for his cousin Toby and keeping him safe while his aunt was away, Matt became more of an adult and less of a child. Taking care of someone else is an adult thing to do and Matt was successful. This was a defining moment in his life.

Comparison of communication in different forms

Some elements to include in a comparison of communication in different forms include aspects of the plot, characterization, and the author's use of language. If one has ever read a story and seen a movie of the same story, it is obvious that the director of the movie will often leave out certain scenes from the book that may not be easily depicted visually. This may change the flow of the story line or emphasize one strand of the plot over another. In addition, characterization may be different in different versions of the same story. Using dialogue differently and shifting the point of view may alter characterization across different forms of communication. The use of figurative language may not be transferred verbatim when a dramatic performance is made based on a print version of a story either. Lastly, a dramatic performance, by its nature, includes a visual element that is lacking in a print story.

Purpose

The four purposes of texts are: to inform, to influence or persuade, to express, and to entertain. Newspaper articles, encyclopedia entries, and functional documents are written to inform; authors give facts and write in an objective tone. Editorials and advertisements are written to influence; authors use persuasive language to try to be convincing. Descriptive paragraphs are written to express something; authors use lots of adjectives to describe objects. Fictional stories and screenplays are written to entertain; authors may use humor or dramatic elements to entertain their audiences.

Example 1

Gorillas are large primates. They live on the ground in the forests of Africa.

The sentences shown here contain factual information about gorillas. The author is not trying to describe the physical appearance of a gorilla or a situation in which a gorilla is doing something interesting. He is not trying to persuade the reader to do anything with regard to gorillas. He is not telling a story about gorillas. Thus, from this deduction, one can determine that the author is writing with the purpose of informing the reader about the gorilla and its habitat.

Example 2

Softsuds is the best shampoo on the market. It will leave your hair tangle-free and shiny. Try it out to see for yourself. Pick some up today.

There are four main purposes an author may have when writing: to inform, to express, to influence, and to entertain. The sentences shown here contain persuasive language about a certain brand of shampoo. The sentences might be used in a commercial or other advertisement. The author is not trying to give factual information about the shampoo. He is not trying to describe the aroma or feeling of the shampoo's lather. The author is not telling a story about an experience using the shampoo either. Thus, from this deduction, one can determine that the author is writing with the purpose of influencing or persuading the reader to use the Softsuds brand of shampoo.

Intertextuality

Intertextuality refers to the interrelationship between two texts, or the shaping of one text's meaning by the other. Intertextuality has come to have several different meanings. It can be used as a stylish way of talking about intertextual figures like allusion, quotation, or translation. Two examples that make use of intertextuality would be an author's borrowing and transformation of a prior text to create a new text, or a reader's referencing of one text while reading another text.

Historical and Cultural Setting

Historical context influences literature in a number of ways. The style of the author's writing can be impacted by the historical period during which it was written (e.g., Dickens wrote at a time when authors were paid by the word; this is why his novels are so long). Obviously, the setting of the book includes its historical context. In addition, dialect may be a function of the historical period of the book. When a reader understands the historical context of a particular book, he or she can have a deeper understanding of the novel. Knowing about the time period in which the author wrote, as well as the time period discussed in the novel, helps the reader understand some of the author's choices, including character motivations.

Example

Slavery used to be the norm in Southern states. One of the major ways in which the historical context of slavery impacted literature coming out of the South was the birth of the slave narrative. Slaves wanted to have their experiences documented. After the Civil War, former slaves wrote their stories. These slave narratives have given historians valuable firsthand accounts of life in the South. From a literary perspective, slave narratives are one of the most important genres of African-American writing. Slavery influenced literature by delving into themes of power, racial injustice, and equality. Literature from this time period can help the reader better understand the perspectives and experiences of the slaves themselves, as well as the slave holders.

Compare and contrast

When an author describes the ways in which two things are alike, he or she is comparing them. When the author describes the ways in which two things are different, he or she is contrasting them. The "compare and contrast" essay is one of the most common forms in nonfiction. It is often signaled with certain words: a comparison may be indicated with such words as both, same, like, too, and as well; while a contrast may be indicated by words like but, however, on the other hand, instead, and yet. Of course, comparisons and contrasts may be implicit without using any such signaling language. A single sentence may both compare and contrast. Consider the sentence Brian and Sheila love ice cream, but Brian prefers vanilla and Sheila prefers strawberry. In one sentence, the author has described both a similarity (love of ice cream) and a difference (favorite flavor).

Epic poetry and lyric poetry

An epic poem is a lengthy, narrative poem that usually tells a story about a serious or heroic deed. These types of poems are important within specific cultures or groups of people. In an epic, the hero tends to go on a journey or a quest. The hero meets many adversaries and enemies along the way. Through each encounter the hero may learn something new. When the hero returns home he has changed significantly through his journey. Most often the hero's trials are related to morals that were important to the specific culture.

Lyric poetry is a type of poetry that expresses the author's personal feelings. This type of poetry is almost always emotional. They author will use sensory language to influence the audience's emotions. Originally, lyric poetry was written to be sung along with a lyre, a type of stringed instrument. It is a type of poetry that doesn't have to rhyme or even be set to music.

Protagonist and antagonist

The protagonist is the main character in a drama, movie, novel, or other fictional text. The antagonist is the character that actively opposes the protagonist. The author portrays the protagonist in a way that the audience is most like to identify with themselves. The protagonist is generally undertaking some type of personal challenge throughout the story, while the antagonist is trying to prevent them from succeeding. The author writes the story so that the reader becomes aware of the protagonist's emotions and is generally able to empathize with the personal challenge. The antagonist is usually presented in such a way as to make the audience dislike them, and want them to fail at stopping the protagonist.

Style, tone, and mood

Authors use language and word choice to convey a certain style, tone, and mood in a piece of literature. When an author writes, he or she uses a style appropriate to the purpose of the text, but also uses language in a way that sets him or her apart. Tone is the author's attitude toward the subject and mood is the feeling the work invokes in the reader. Authors use their own personal style, their attitude toward the subject, and the mood they create to help craft their stories. Style, tone, and mood all contribute to the effect of a text. As readers, we know there is a difference between a serious or humorous piece, for example.

Plot line

Every plot line follows the same stages. One can identify each of these stages in every story they read. These stages are: the introduction, rising action, conflict, climax, falling action, and resolution. The introduction tells the reader what the story will be about and sets up the plot. The rising action is what happens that leads up to the conflict, which is some sort of problem that arises, with the climax at its peak. The falling action is what happens after the climax of the conflict. The resolution is the conclusion and often has the final solution to the problem in the conflict.

A plot line looks like this:

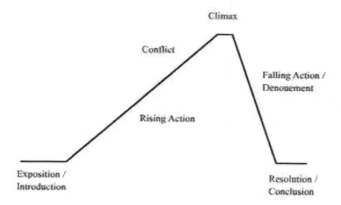

Common characteristics in literature

Some common characteristics found in all genres of literary text, from historical fiction to fables, include character, plot, conflict/resolution, and setting. The characters are the people who do the action in the story. The plot is the storyline and generally includes a conflict, or problem, and its resolution, or the way that the main character solves the problem in the story. The setting is the time and place where the story takes place.

Character analysis

When one analyzes a character, one should pay attention to the character's physical traits, thoughts, feelings and attitudes, and motivations. Physical traits include any description of how the character appears, for example, this can include hair and eye color, height, and clothing. The character's thoughts, feelings, and attitudes include his or her ideas about certain topics or other characters in the story. The character's motivations are the reasons why he or she behaves a certain way. For example, in a mystery novel, the protagonist may act in a deceitful way toward a suspect but the motivation for doing so may be to gain information and uncover the truth. This lets the reader understand that even though the character acts in a deceitful way, he or she is not a bad person. The motivation allows the reader to better understand the character and their actions.

Point of view

The point of view of a text is the perspective from which it is told. Every literary text has a narrator, or person who tells the story. The two main points of view that authors use are first person and third person. If the narrator is also the main character, or protagonist, of a work, it is written in first person point of view. In first person, the author writes with the word, "I" and gives the reader insights into all of their thoughts and opinions. Third person point of view is probably the most common. Using third person, authors refer to each character using "he" or "she." In third person omniscient, the narrator is not a character in the story and can tell the story of all of the characters at the same time, often revealing their thoughts and opinions as they become relevant.

Authors' choose which point of view they want to use in their text in order to best achieve their purpose. For example, using first person point of view can make a story seem more intimate, but the reader only sees the story line from the perspective of the narrator. If a writer wants the reader to understand the motivations of more than one character, he or she would use third person omniscient narrative. This is an overall narrative where the reader sees everything happening in the story, often with insights into multiple characters' minds.

When a story is written from the first person point of view, it is told from the point of view of the narrator, who is often the main character, or protagonist. The story is told using the pronouns "I" and "me." When a story is told from one character's point of view, the scope is limited to what that character thinks and knows and the story carries that character's biases; it is not a broad telling of the story from an outside and objective narrator. Regardless, an author might choose to use first person point of view because it can be very intimate. The reader feels very close to the protagonist and understands the situation from his or her perspective.

<u>Example</u>

Read the following excerpt from Jane Austen's <u>Emma</u> and discuss the point of view:

"Doing just what she liked; highly esteeming Miss Taylor's judgments, but directed chiefly by her own. The real evils, indeed, of Emma's situation were the power of having rather too much her own way, and a disposition to think a little too well of herself."

In order to determine the point of view, one should first look at the pronouns used in the passage. If the passage has the pronoun "I" it is probably written in first person point of view, in which the protagonist is the narrator. In the case of this excerpt, a narrator who is not the protagonist is telling the story. The pronouns used are "she" and "her" which are clues that someone is talking about the character rather than the character speaking for herself, indicating it is written in the third person point of view. An outside narrator is telling the story *about* Emma, she is not telling the story about herself.

Figurative language

Figurative language refers to a number of ways writers deviate from literal meaning in text. Some forms of figurative language include similes, extended metaphors, aphorisms, and epigraphs. A simile shows the similarity between two ideas or objects, using the words like or as to draw a comparison. An extended metaphor, also known as a conceit or sustained metaphor, is when an author exploits a single metaphor or analogy at length throughout all or a large part of a text. An aphorism is a short phrase that expresses a truth or wise idea, such as the saying "If it ain't broke, don't fix it." An epigraph is a brief motto or quotation set at the beginning of a text to suggest its theme.

Inference

An inference is a conclusion that the reader makes using clues in the text. In a fictional work of literature, there are things that the author does not explicitly mention, but hints at; the reader needs to connect the dots of these clues to draw a conclusion. This is called making an inference. An inference is different from making a guess, as an inference is based on evidence; the reader needs to use specific textual evidence to make the inference. For example, an author might mention that a character has a messy room and papers falling out of his binder. The reader can infer that the character is sloppy and disorganized even though the author does not explicitly state this fact.

Example 1

An inference can be made about the character of the narrator based on the following excerpt from David Copperfield by Charles Dickens:

My father's eyes had closed upon the light of this world six months, when mine opened on it. There is something strange to me...in the shadowy remembrance that I have of my first childish associations with his white grave-stone in the churchyard, and of the indefinable compassion I used to feel for it lying out alone there in the dark night, when our little parlour was warm and bright with fire and candle, and the doors of our house were - almost cruelly, it seemed to me sometimes - bolted and locked against it.

In order to make an inference, the reader must use clues from the passage to come to a conclusion. It is explicitly stated in the passage that David's father died before he was born. Based on the excerpt, the reader can infer that David Copperfield feels sadness over the loss of his father, even though he never knew him. This inference about David's character can be made using context clues from the passage: David feels "indefinable compassion" for his father's gravestone. The phrase "almost cruelly" indicates that David feels that his family is perhaps too harsh in their treatment of his father. He feels a connection to his father's gravestone and feels bad that the stone is left out in the cold when his house is warm.

Example 2

An inference can be made about the character Pip based on the following excerpt from Great Expectations by Charles Dickens:

I never had one hour's happiness in her society, and yet my mind all round the four-and-twenty hours was harping on the happiness of having her with me unto death.

In order to make an inference, the reader must use clues from the passage to come to a conclusion. This excerpt shows the reader Pip, who is thinking about a romantic relationship with a woman. The words "yet my mind all round the four and twenty hours" and "harping" lead the reader to infer that he has a crush on this woman and cannot get her out of his thoughts. Pip has never enjoyed her company, yet he dreams of their happiness together. From this, the reader can infer that Pip is unrealistic about romantic relationships.

Media

Media are methods of storing or delivering information. Mass media is a type of media, such as television, radio, or the internet, that conveys information to the general public, or the masses. Print media is a type of media that includes any printed documents, such as this study material, used to transmit information. News media is a type of mass media that includes newspapers, newsletters, television news shows, and other means of transmitting news. Another widely used type is advertising media. This includes television and radio commercials, billboards, and newspaper ads. In many cases, media are used not only to convey information, but also to affect opinion and action. For instance in advertising, the advertiser conveys biased opinions about a product, hoping to profit from the recipient of the information buying the advertised product. News media should be unbiased, but opinions can be very easily intermixed with fact, such that an undiscerning recipient may not be able to distinguish between the fact and opinion, and simply accept both as fact.

Textual evidence

Using textual evidence means referring to specific things mentioned within the text when talking about it. When one discusses a text, they want to use textual evidence to make their argument or statement stronger. Using textual evidence helps support the argument being made and gives what is being said more weight. By quoting from the text or mentioning specific details the author used, one can better support the argument they are making. An argument will be weak and unconvincing if one does not provide support; including facts, details, and evidence from texts read.

Paraphrasing and summarizing

Paraphrasing and summarizing are two methods one can use to help them understand what they read. When paraphrasing, one puts what they have read into their own words, rephrasing what the author has written to make it their own, to "translate" all of what the author says to their own words, including as many details as they can. When summarizing, on the other hand, one does not include many details, but rather simply the main idea of the text. Often times, a summary can be done in just one sentence, boiling down the author's words into just main idea.

<u>Example summary</u>
Read the following paragraph and then give a one sentence summary statement:

People used to know their bankers. Now, many people do their banking online. With a login and password, customers can have access to their accounts with up to the minute information. Users can keep track of their spending, transfer money between accounts, and pay bills online, all from the comfort of home.

In order to summarize, one has to identify the main idea and any supporting ideas in the author's work. The summary is an overview of the author's paragraph and will tell what it is about without getting into any of the details. The summary needs to be broad enough to cover all of the information in the author's paragraph. Here is a possible summary statement for the above paragraph:

Most people nowadays find it convenient to do their banking online instead of at a branch office.

<u>Example paraphrasing</u>
Read the following sentences and then paraphrase the material:

The government is debating a new health care system for our country. The Senate and the House of Representatives have both passed bills; now they need to resolve these two bills into one bill that a majority can agree on.

When paraphrasing information, one needs to read carefully and pay attention to details, then put the material away and write or tell it in their own words. One does not want to look at the material while paraphrasing to avoid plagiarizing by accident. Here is one example of a way to paraphrase the sentences:

Our government is trying to adopt a new health care system. The Senate has passed a bill and so has the House of Representatives. Their bills are different so now they have to compromise on one bill that can be passed.

Synthesizing a text

Synthesizing is similar to summarizing but it takes it one step further. Synthesizing involves taking the main points of a text and comparing it with existing knowledge to create a new idea, perspective, or way of thinking. Instead of using existing knowledge, synthesizing may instead be done by combining the ideas provided in two or three different texts. The reader must make connections between the texts, determine how the ideas fit together, and gather evidence to support the new perspective.

Rhetorical and logical fallacies

A rhetorical fallacy, or a fallacy of argument, does not allow the open, two-way exchange of ideas upon which meaningful conversations exist. A logical fallacy, by contrast, refers to an error in reasoning. Examples of fallacies include loaded terms, caricatures, leading questions, false assumptions, and incorrect premises. A loaded term is wording that attempts to influence the reader with an appeal to emotion or stereotype. These words or phrases have strong positive or negative reactions beyond their literal meaning. A caricature is a description of a person using either exaggerated or over simplified characteristics. A leading question is one that is asked in such a way as to suggest at a particular answer. For example, the question "Didn't you think the football game on Saturday was boring?" is a leading question that could be asked in a non-leading way as "What did you think of the football game on Saturday?" False assumptions are based on a distorted view of factual information. A person may see the facts but then they bend them to fit their own needs. An incorrect premise, or false premise, is an incorrect proposition that forms the basis of an argument.

Evaluating graphics

Texts can contain a variety of graphics and it is up to the reader to evaluate the graphic for clarity and decide if it achieves its purpose. One example of a graphic that is commonly used in a compare and contrast text is a Venn diagram. A Venn diagram is a graphic organizer composed of two (or more) interlocking circles. It is best used to represent information where two items are being compared and contrasted. Facts and details about one item can be written in one circle (i.e., the green area on the left in the diagram below) and facts and details about the second item are written in the second circle (i.e., the purple area on the right in the diagram below). In the overlapping space of the two circles (i.e., the middle portion in the diagram below), facts and details that are true of both items are written. In this way, it is easy to see the similarities and differences between two (or more) things.

Bar and line graph

When selecting a graph format, it is important to consider the intention and the structure of the presentation. A bar graph, for instance, is appropriate for displaying the relations between a series of distinct quantities that are on the same scale. For instance, if one wanted to display the amount of money spent on groceries during the months of a year, a bar graph would be appropriate. The vertical axis would represent values of money, and the horizontal axis would identify the bar representing each month. A line graph also requires data expressed in common units, but it is better for demonstrating the general trend in that data. If the grocery expenses were plotted on a line graph instead of a bar graph, there would be more emphasis on whether the amount of money spent rose or fell over the course of the year. Whereas a bar graph is good for showing the relationships between the different values plotted, the line graph is good for showing whether the values tended to increase, decrease, or remain stable.

Fact and opinion

A fact is something that is said about a subject that can be tested and proved to be true. Examples of facts include details and statistics. For example, a fact could be:

1. That balloon is red.
2. 85% of the kids in the class do not get enough sleep.

Since both of these can be proven true, they should be identified as facts. An opinion, on the other hand, is what someone thinks about a subject. An opinion cannot be tested or proven to be true because it is subjective. One person may think one thing and another person something the complete opposite. Examples of opinions include thoughts, beliefs, and ideas. For instance, an opinion could be:

1. The colors used to paint the house make it look welcoming and inviting.
2. I believe that the school leadership team is acting effectively.

Authors use certain phrases to state opinions and it is important for a reader to be able to identify the author's opinion about a subject. The reader can use these phrases to help identify as an opinion, as opposed to a fact. Some phrases that indicate an opinion statement include: 'I believe,' 'I think,' 'in my opinion,' 'it seems to me,' 'it's obvious that,' 'it's clear that,' and 'they should.'

It is important that a reader be able to distinguish between a fact and an opinion. A fact is something said about a subject that can be tested and proved to be true. Examples of facts include details and statistics. An opinion is what someone thinks about a subject and cannot be tested or proven to be true, as it is subjective. One person may think one thing and another person the exact opposite. Examples of opinions include thoughts, beliefs, and ideas. The reader needs to be able to identify if something is true or merely the author's opinion in order to determine whether or not to trust the source. When something is presented factually, the reader can trust the source to be accurate and unbiased. When information presented is the author's opinion, the reader can decide for him- or herself whether or not to agree with the author.

Organizational methods to structure text

Authors organize their writing based on the purpose of their text. Some common organizational methods that authors use include: cause and effect, compare/contrast, inductive presentation of ideas, deductive presentation of ideas, and chronological order. Cause and effect is used to present the reason why something happened. Compare/contrast is used to discuss the similarities and differences between two things. Inductive presentation of ideas starts with specific examples and moves to a general conclusion. Deductive presentation of ideas starts with a general conclusion, then explains the examples used to arrive at the conclusion. Chronological order presents information in the order that it occurred.

Cause and effect and chronological order

Authors have to organize information logically so the reader can follow it and locate information within the text. Two common organizational structures are *cause and effect* and *chronological order*. In *cause and effect*, an author presents one thing that makes something else happen. For example, if one were to go to bed very late, they would be tired. The cause is going to bed late, with the effect of being tired the next day. When using *chronological order*, the author presents information in the order that it happened. For example, biographies are written in chronological order; the subject's birth and childhood are presented first, followed by their adult life, and lastly by the events leading up to the person's death.

Example

Read the following thesis statement and discuss the organizational pattern the author will use:

While many people are content with the DVD players they already have at home, Blu-ray technology provides for better viewing of high definition video.

From this thesis statement the reader can assume that the author is going to use a deductive presentation of ideas. The author starts with the conclusion that Blu-ray technology is a better method for watching high definition video than DVD. The reader can assume that in the rest of the text, the author will discuss the reasons why he arrived at this conclusion, most likely providing details and examples that will support his conclusion. When the conclusion is presented first, then followed by specific examples, the ideas are presented in deductive order.

Example

Read the following thesis statement and discuss the organizational pattern that the author will use:

Among people who are current on the latest technologies, there is a debate over whether DVD or Blu-ray Disc is a better choice for watching and recording video.

From the thesis statement the reader can assume that the author is going to use a compare/ contrast organizational structure. The author mentions two options for watching and recording video: DVD and Blu-ray Disc. During the rest of the essay, the author will most likely describe the two technologies, giving specific examples of how they are similar and the differences that set them apart. The compare/ contrast structure is best used to discuss they similarities and differences of two things.

Example

Read the following thesis statement and discuss the organizational pattern that the author will use:

Throughout his life, Thomas Edison used his questioning and creative mind to become one of America's greatest inventors.

Based on the thesis statement, the reader can assume that the author is going to use chronological order to organize the information in the rest of the essay. The words "throughout his life" clue the reader in to the chronological organizational structure, which presents information in the order than it occurred. The author will probably discuss Edison's childhood and initial inventions first and then move on to his later queries and inventions. Chronological order is often used as the organizational structure in biographies as a way to logically present the important events in a person's life.

Outline

<u>Example</u>

Write a brief outline for a paragraph on large cats that will include information on the habitat and food for lions, tigers, cheetahs, and leopards.

In the paragraph described, one can break the topic into four brief sections, one for each animal. The subsections for each can be their habitat and food. Here is an example outline:

1. Large Cats
   a. Lions
      i. Habitat
      ii. Food
   b. Tigers
      i. Habitat
      ii. Food
   c. Cheetahs
      i. Habitat
      ii. Food
   d. Leopards
      i. Habitat
      ii. Food

Elements in a written response to literature

A written response to literature is one's response or reaction to a certain piece of text. When one responds to text, they should include their background knowledge on the topic, connections they can make to their own life, connections they can make to other texts they have read, and what the text makes them feel and think about. One may also include ways that they agree or disagree with the author and questions they may have for the author. Using specific evidence (i.e., quotes) from the text can support and strengthen a response.

Reading Practice Test #1

Questions 1 -12 pertain to the following passages:

Call of the Wild by Jack London

(1) Buck did not read the newspapers, or he would have known that trouble was brewing, not alone for himself, but for every tide-water dog, strong of muscle and with warm, long hair, from Puget Sound to San Diego. Because men, groping in the Arctic darkness, had found a yellow metal, and because steamship and transportation companies were booming the find, thousands of men were rushing into the Northland. These men wanted dogs, and the dogs they wanted were heavy dogs, with strong muscles by which to toil, and furry coats to protect them from the frost.

(2) Buck lived at a big house in the sun-kissed Santa Clara Valley. Judge Miller's place, it was called. It stood back from the road, half hidden among the trees, through which glimpses could be caught of the wide cool veranda that ran around its four sides. The house was approached by gravelled driveways which wound about through wide-spreading lawns and under the interlacing boughs of tall poplars. At the rear things were on even a more spacious scale than at the front. There were great stables, where a dozen grooms and boys held forth, rows of vine-clad servants' cottages, an endless and orderly array of outhouses, long grape arbors, green pastures, orchards, and berry patches. Then there was the pumping plant for the artesian well, and the big cement tank where Judge Miller's boys took their morning plunge and kept cool in the hot afternoon.

(3) And over this great demesne Buck ruled. Here he was born, and here he had lived the four years of his life. It was true, there were other dogs, There could not but be other dogs on so vast a place, but they did not count. They came and went, resided in the populous kennels, or lived obscurely in the recesses of the house after the fashion of Toots, the Japanese pug, or Ysabel, the Mexican hairless,—strange creatures that rarely put nose out of doors or set foot to ground. On the other hand, there were the fox terriers, a score of them at least, who yelped fearful promises at Toots and Ysabel looking out of the windows at them and protected by a legion of housemaids armed with brooms and mops.

(4) But Buck was neither house-dog nor kennel-dog. The whole realm was his. He plunged into the swimming tank or went hunting with the Judge's sons; he escorted Mollie and Alice, the Judge's daughters, on long twilight or early morning rambles; on wintry nights he lay at the Judge's feet before the roaring library fire; he carried the Judge's grandsons on his back, or rolled them in the grass, and guarded their footsteps through wild adventures down to the fountain in the stable yard, and even beyond, where the paddocks were, and the berry patches. Among the terriers he stalked imperiously, and Toots and Ysabel he utterly ignored, for he was king,—king over all creeping, crawling, flying things of Judge Miller's place, humans included.

(5) His father, Elmo, a huge St. Bernard, had been the Judge's inseparable companion, and Buck bid fair to follow in the way of his father. He was not so large,—he weighed only one hundred and forty pounds,—for his mother, Shep, had been a Scotch shepherd dog. Nevertheless, one hundred and forty pounds, to which was added the dignity that comes of good living and universal respect, enabled him to carry himself in right royal fashion. During the four years since his puppyhood he had lived the life of a sated aristocrat; he had

- 29 -

a fine pride in himself, was even a trifle egotistical, as country gentlemen sometimes become because of their insular situation. But he had saved himself by not becoming a mere pampered house-dog. Hunting and kindred outdoor delights had kept down the fat and hardened his muscles; and to him, as to the cold-tubbing races, the love of water had been a tonic and a health preserver.

(6) And this was the manner of dog Buck was in the fall of 1897, when the Klondike strike dragged men from all the world into the frozen North. But Buck did not read the newspapers, and he did not know that Manuel, one of the gardener's helpers, was an undesirable acquaintance. Manuel had one besetting sin. He loved to play Chinese lottery. Also, in his gambling, he had one besetting weakness—faith in a system; and this made his damnation certain. For to play a system requires money, while the wages of a gardener's helper do not lap over the needs of a wife and numerous progeny.

(7) The Judge was at a meeting of the Raisin Growers' Association, and the boys were busy organizing an athletic club, on the memorable night of Manuel's treachery. No one saw him and Buck go off through the orchard on what Buck imagined was merely a stroll. And with the exception of a solitary man, no one saw them arrive at the little flag station known as College Park. This man talked with Manuel, and money chinked between them.

(8) "You might wrap up the goods before you deliver 'm," the stranger said gruffly, and Manuel doubled a piece of stout rope around Buck's neck under the collar.

1. What is the purpose of paragraphs 2-5?

   a. To introduce all of the story's characters
   b. To show Buck's personality
   c. To introduce Buck
   d. To show Buck's affection for Toots and Ysabel

2. Which sentence or phrase shows Buck's attitude about Judge Miller's place?

   a. They came and went, resided in the populous kennels, or lived obscurely in the recesses of the house
   b. The whole realm was his
   c. He had a fine pride in himself
   d. And to him, as to the cold-tubbing races, the love of water had been a tonic and a health preserver

3. The author uses the detail in paragraph 1 to

   a. Describe Buck's life
   b. Foreshadow Buck's story
   c. Describe the story's setting
   d. Introduce the story's villain

4. What is the significance of the Klondike strike in 1897?

   a. It will lead to changes in Buck's life
   b. It will cause more dogs to move to Judge Miller's place
   c. It changed Elmo's life
   d. It caused the Raisin Growers' Association to meet more frequently

5. The use of the word *imperiously* in paragraph four helps the reader know that Buck feels
    a. Scared
    b. Angry
    c. Happy
    d. Regal

6. The author organizes this selection mainly by
    a. Describing Buck's life in the order in which it happened
    b. Outlining Buck's history
    c. Showing Buck's life and then showing a moment of change
    d. Comparing Buck's life at Judge Miller's place to what came afterwards

7. Which answer choice best describes the purpose of the selection?
    a. To set up a story by providing background information
    b. To show Buck in a moment of heroism
    c. To give details about the Klondike strike
    d. To introduce all the dogs that live at Judge Miller's

8. In the future, Buck will probably
    a. Continue to act like the king of Judge Miller's place
    b. Reunite with his father, Elmo, and his mother, Shep
    c. Leave Judge Miller's place against his will
    d. Spend more time in the garden

9. This selection is part of a longer work. Based on the selection, what might be a theme of the larger work?
    a. Change
    b. Family
    c. Hard work
    d. Relationships

10. Paragraph 2 is mostly about:
    a. The Santa Clara Valley
    b. Judge Miller's place
    c. Buck's lifestyle
    d. The Klondike strike

11. Which sentence from the passage foreshadows the rest of the story?
    a. And over this great demesne Buck ruled
    b. These men wanted dogs, and the dogs they wanted were heavy dogs, with strong muscles by which to toil, and furry coats to protect them from the frost
    c. His father, Elmo, a huge St. Bernard, had been the Judge's inseparable companion and Buck bid fair to follow in the way of his father
    d. But he had saved himself by not becoming a mere pampered house-dog

12. What's the most logical explanation why Buck doesn't read the newspapers?

    a. He's not interested in current events

    b. He's busy exploring Judge Miller's place

    c. The Raisin Growers' Association takes all his time

    d. He's a dog

Questions 13 – 16 pertain to the following passage:

Andy Grant's Pluck by Horatio Alger

(1) The house and everything about it seemed just as it did when he left at the beginning of the school term. But Andy looked at them with different eyes.

(2) Then he had been in good spirits, eager to return to his school work.

Now something had happened, he did not yet know what.

(3) Mrs. Grant was in the back part of the house, and Andy was in the sitting room before she was fully aware of his presence. Then she came in from the kitchen, where she was preparing supper.

(4) Her face seemed careworn, but there was a smile upon it as she greeted her son.

(5) "Then you got my telegram?" she said. "I didn't think you would be here so soon."

(6) "I started at once, mother, for I felt anxious. What has happened? Are you all well?"

(7) "Yes, thank God, we are in fair health, but we have met with misfortune."

(8) "What is it?"

(9) "Nathan Lawrence, cashier of the bank in Benton, has disappeared with twenty thousand dollars of the bank's money."

(10) "What has that to do with father? He hasn't much money in that bank."

(11) "Your father is on Mr. Lawrence's bond to the amount of six thousand dollars."

(12) "I see," answered Andy, gravely, "How much will he lose?"

(13) "The whole of it."

(14) This, then, was what had happened. To a man in moderate circumstances, it must needs be a heavy blow.

(15) "I suppose it will make a great difference?" said Andy, inquiringly.

(16) "You can judge. Your father's property consists of this farm and three thousand dollars in government bonds. It will be necessary to sacrifice the bonds and place a mortgage of three thousand dollars on the farm."

(17) "How much is the farm worth?"

(18) "Not over six thousand dollars."

(19) "Then father's property is nearly all swept away."

(20) "Yes," said his mother, sadly. "Hereafter he will receive no help from outside interest, and will, besides, have to pay interest on a mortgage of three thousand dollars, at six per cent."

(21) "One hundred and eighty dollars."

(22) "Yes."

(23) "Altogether, then, it will diminish our income by rather more than three hundred dollars."

(24) "Yes, Andy."

(25) "That is about what my education has been costing father," said Andy, in a low voice.

(26) He began to see how this misfortune was going to affect him.

(27) "I am afraid," faltered Mrs. Grant, "that you will have to leave school."

(28) "Of course I must," said Andy, speaking with a cheerfulness which he did not feel. "And in place of going to college I must see how I can help father bear this burden."

(29) "It will be very hard upon you, Andy," said his mother, in a tone of sympathy.

(30) "I shall be sorry, of course, mother; but there are plenty of boys who don't go to college. I shall be no worse off than they."

(31) "I am glad you bear the disappointment so well, Andy. It is of you your father and I have thought chiefly since the blow fell upon us."

(32) "Who will advance father the money on mortgage, mother?"

(33) "Squire Carter has expressed a willingness to do so. He will be here this evening to talk it over."

(34) "I am sorry for that, mother. He is a hard man. If there is a chance to take advantage of father, he won't hesitate to do it."

13. As it used in paragraph 1, the phrase *different eyes* means which of the following?
   a. Andy's eyes have changed color
   b. Andy now wears glasses
   c. Andy sees that the mood in the house has changed
   d. Andy is happy to be home

14. Read this sentence from paragraph 14:

To a man in moderate circumstances, it must needs be a heavy blow.

The author uses the metaphor *a heavy blow* to indicate which of the following?

    a. Andy's father is in a difficult situation
    b. Andy won't be able to go back to school
    c. Andy's father has lost over six thousand dollars
    d. Andy is disappointed about his family's problems

15. Which of these is the best summary of the selection?

    a. Andy Grant comes home from school and discovers that his father has won six thousand dollars. He will use the money to buy equipment for the farm. Andy finds out that he will need to leave school in order to help his father on the farm and work for Squire Carter
    b. Andy Grant goes home and discovers that his family has fallen upon misfortune. Nathan Lawrence, the bank's cashier, has stolen twenty thousand dollars of Andy's father's money. Now that Andy's family has lost so much money, they won't be able to pay for his education and he'll have to leave school
    c. Andy Grant's father has lost six thousand dollars because Nathan Lawrence stole it. This loss will cost Andy's family a lot of money. Since Andy's family pays $300 a month for his school, he will have to stop going to school. Andy is very cheerful that he doesn't have to go to school. He decides to work for Squire Carter in order to help his family
    d. Andy Grant's family has suffered a misfortune because the bank's cashier stole money, some of which belonged to Andy's father. Without the money, Andy's family will have trouble paying its bills, including Andy's school bills. Andy will have to stop going to school. Furthermore, his father will have to borrow money

16. What phrase or sentence from the selection best shows Andy's feelings about having to leave school?

    a. He began to see how this misfortune was going to affect him
    b. Speaking with a cheerfulness which he did not feel
    c. And in place of going to college I must see how I can help father bear this burden
    d. I am sorry for that, mother

Questions 17 – 21 pertain to the following passage:

The Telegraph Boy by Horatio Alger

(1) Our hero found himself in a dirty apartment, provided with a bar, over which was a placard, inscribed:—

(2) "FREE LUNCH."

(3) "How much money have you got, Frank?" inquired Montagu Percy.

(4) "Twenty-five cents."

(5) "Lunch at this establishment is free," said Montagu; "but you are expected to order some drink. What will you have?"

(6) "I don't care for any drink except a glass of water."

(7) "All right; I will order for you, as the rules of the establishment require it; but I will drink your glass myself. Eat whatever you like."

(8) Frank took a sandwich from a plate on the counter and ate it with relish, for he was hungry. Meanwhile his companion emptied the two glasses, and ordered another.

(9) "Can you pay for these drinks?" asked the bar-tender, suspiciously.

(10) "Sir, I never order what I cannot pay for."

(11) "I don't know about that. You've been in here and taken lunch more than once without drinking anything."

(12) "It may be so. I will make up for it now. Another glass, please."

(13) "First pay for what you have already drunk."

(14) "Frank, hand me your money," said Montagu.

(15) Frank incautiously handed him his small stock of money, which he saw instantly transferred to the bar-tender.

(16) "That is right, I believe," said Montagu Percy.

(17) The bar-keeper nodded, and Percy, transferring his attention to the free lunch, stowed away a large amount.

(18) Frank observed with some uneasiness the transfer of his entire cash capital to the bar-tender; but concluded that Mr. Percy would refund a part after they went out. As they reached the street he broached the subject.

(19) "I didn't agree to pay for both dinners," he said, uneasily.

(20) "Of course not. It will be my treat next time. That will be fair, won't it?"

(21) "But I would rather you would give me back a part of my money. I may not see you again."

(22) "I will be in the Park to-morrow at one o'clock."

(23) "Give me back ten cents, then," said Frank, uneasily. "That was all the money I had."

(24) "I am really sorry, but I haven't a penny about me. I'll make it right to-morrow. Good-day, my young friend. Be virtuous and you will be happy."

(25) Frank looked after the shabby figure ruefully. He felt that he had been taken in and done for. His small capital had vanished, and he was adrift in the streets of a strange city without a penny.

17. Why did Frank give Mr. Percy all his money?
   a. He was feeling generous
   b. Mr. Percy offered to pay for the sandwiches
   c. He owed it to Mr. Percy
   d. He thought Mr. Percy would give him some of it back

18. What does the phrase "his small capital" mean in paragraph 25?

    a. Frank's penny
    b. Frank's twenty-five cents
    c. Frank's virtuous nature
    d. Frank's friendship with Mr. Percy

19. Why did Frank agree to eat lunch?

    a. Mr. Percy was paying for it
    b. Lunch was completely free
    c. He only needed to buy a drink
    d. He wanted to spend time with Mr. Percy

20. Is Mr. Percy likely to pay Frank back?

    a. Yes, because he never orders what he cannot pay for
    b. Yes, because he will be in the Park the next day at one o'clock
    c. No, because Frank is not virtuous or happy
    d. No, because he's shown that he does not have any money

21. What adjective best describes Frank's feelings in paragraph 25?

    a. Disappointed
    b. Incautious
    c. Uneasy
    d. Suspicious

Questions 22 – 25 pertain to both "Andy Grant's Pluck" and "The Telegraph Boy passages":

22. How are Andy and Frank similar?

    a. They both have loving families
    b. They both have experienced misfortune
    c. They both were tricked
    d. They both need money for food

23. How are "Andy Grant's Pluck" and "The Telegraph Boy" different?

    a. "Andy Grant's Pluck" explains the circumstances that led to Andy's family misfortune, and "The Telegraph Boy" does not explain how Frank ended up with no money at all
    b. Andy is all alone, but Frank has many friends who can help him
    c. In "Andy Grant's Pluck," Andy is the victim of his family's bad luck but Frank in "The Telegraph Boy" is in trouble because he lost his own money
    d. "Andy Grant's Pluck" is about how Andy was tricked, and "The Telegraph Boy" is about how Frank lost his money

24. Both selections end with the main characters

    a. Feeling hopeful about the future
    b. Looking forward to going back to school
    c. In a dangerous situation
    d. Feeling uncertain about the future

25. Which of these sentences or phrases from "Andy Grant's Pluck" could also describe how Frank in the "The Telegraph Boy" feels at the end of the selection?

    a. He will receive no help from outside interest
    b. I must see how I can help father bear this burden
    c. Speaking with a cheerfulness which he did not feel
    d. We have met with misfortune

Questions 26 -31 pertain to the following passage:

The Great Round World and What is Going On In It by William Beverley Harison

(1) There is a new cause for supposing that the Treaty with Great Britain will either be defeated in the Senate, or else delayed for some time to come.

(2) This new trouble concerns the building of the Nicaragua Canal.

(3) It seems a remote cause, does it not? but it only shows how closely the affairs of one nation are bound up with those of all the others. No matter what our speech, our climate, or our color, we are all a portion of the great human family, and the good of one is the good of all.

(4) The Nicaragua Canal is a water-way that will cross the narrow neck of land that makes Central America. It will connect the Atlantic Ocean with the Pacific Ocean.

(5) With the help of such a canal, ships in going to the western coast of North or South America will not need to make the long and dangerous voyage around Cape Horn.

(6) Cape Horn, you will see if you look on your map, is the extreme southerly point of South America.

(7) There are so many storms and fogs there, that the Horn, as it is called, is much dreaded by sailors.

(8) Since the invention of steam, all the steamships go through the Straits of Magellan, and save the passage round the Horn; but there is not enough wind for sailing vessels in the rocky and narrow straits, so they still have to take the outside passage.

(9) The Straits of Magellan divide the main continent of South America from a group of islands, called Tierra del Fuego, and Cape Horn is the most southerly point of this archipelago.

(10) The journey down the coast of South America on the east, and up again on the west, takes such a long time, that the desire for a canal across the narrow neck of land which joins North and South America has been in men's minds for many years.

(11) A railway was built across the Isthmus of Panama to shorten the distance, and save taking the passage round the Horn. Travellers left their ship at one side of the Isthmus, and took the train over to the other, where they went on board another ship, which would take them the rest of their journey.

(12) This plan greatly increased the expense of the journey, and the canal was still so much wanted, that at last the Panama Canal was begun.

(13) You have all heard about the Panama Canal, which was to do the same work that the Nicaragua Canal is to do, that is, to connect the Atlantic and Pacific Oceans. You have probably heard how much time, labor, and human life was wasted over it, and how much trouble its failure caused in France.

(14) This Canal was to cut across the Isthmus at its very narrowest point. It was worked on for years, every one believing that it would be opened to ships before very long. Many of the maps and geographies that were printed in the eighties said that the Panama Canal would be opened in 1888, or at latest in 1889.

(15) No one expected what afterward happened. In 1889 the works were stopped for want of money; the affairs of the Canal were looked into; it was found that there had been dishonesty and fraud, and in 1892 the great Count Ferdinand de Lesseps, who built the Suez Canal, and a number of other prominent Frenchmen, were arrested for dealing dishonestly with the money subscribed for the Canal.

(16) There was a dreadful scandal; many of the high French officials had to give up their positions, and run away for fear of arrest.

(17) When the whole matter was understood, it was found that, for months before the work was stopped, the men who had charge of the Canal had decided that the work would cost such an enormous sum of money that it would be almost an impossibility to complete it.

(18) They did not have the honesty to let this be known, but allowed people to go on subscribing money, a part of which they put in their own pockets, and spent the rest in bribing the French newspapers not to tell the truth about the Canal.

(19) The worst of it was, that the money which had been subscribed was not from rich people, who would feel its loss very little, but from poor people, who put their savings, and the money they were storing away for their old age, into the Canal; and when they lost it, it meant misery and poverty to them.

(20) So the Panama Canal failed.

(21) But the project of making a canal was not given up. Two years before the idea of digging at Panama had been thought of, the ground where the Nicaragua Canal is being built had been surveyed, and thought better suited to the purpose than Panama.

(22) The reason for this was, that at Panama a long and deep cut had to be made through the mountains. This had to be done by blasting, in much the same way that the rocks are cleared away to build houses. This is a long and tedious work.

(23) The Nicaragua Canal will be 159 miles long, while the Panama, if it is ever completed, will be only 59 miles; but of these 159 miles, 117 are through the Nicaragua Lake and the San Juan River—water-ways already made by nature. For the remaining distance, there are other river-beds that will be used, and only 21 miles will actually have to be cut through.

(24) The main objection to this route for the Canal is, that there is a volcano on an island in the Nicaragua Lake, and there are always fears of eruptions and earthquakes in the neighborhood of volcanoes. A great eruption of the volcano might change the course of a river, or alter the face of the country so much, that the Canal might have to be largely remade.

26. The author mentions the treaty with Great Britain in paragraph 1 because people are concerned about

    a. A canal through Cape Horn
    b. The new Panama Canal
    c. The building of the Nicaragua Canal
    d. The Central America Canal

27. What are paragraphs 15-19 mostly about?

    a. The building of the Suez Canal
    b. The financial problems that ended the Panama Canal project
    c. The French newspapers, which did not tell the truth about the canal
    d. Ferdinand de Lesseps' experience in jail

28. Which sentence best shows the purpose for building the Nicaragua Canal?

    a. The new trouble concerns the building of the Nicaragua Canal
    b. Cape Horn, you will see if you look on your map, is the extreme southerly point of South America
    c. There are so many storms and fogs there, that the Horn, as it is called, is much dreaded by sailors
    d. Since the invention of steam, all the steamships go through the Straits of Magellan

29. What is the tone of this passage?

    a. Informational
    b. Humorous
    c. Mysterious
    d. Angry

30. Why will the Nicaragua Canal be easier to build than the Panama Canal?

    a. It is 100 miles longer than the Panama Canal
    b. It needs to be blasted through the mountains
    c. The San Juan River is already a complete canal
    d. Most of the canal will go through existing waterways

31. Look at the time line below.

Canals Around the World

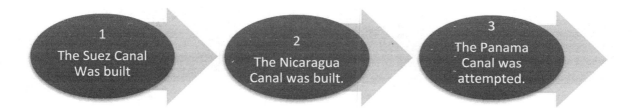

According to the passage, what is the correct order of the time line?

    a. No change
    b. 1, 3, 2
    c. 2, 1, 3
    d. 3, 1, 2

32. The author probably wrote this selection to
    a. Argue against the building of the Nicaragua Canal
    b. Argue for the building of the Nicaragua Canal
    c. Explain the problems that ended the Panama Canal project
    d. Discuss new plans for a canal

33. Which words in paragraph 22 help the reader know what *blasting* means?
    a. Long and deep cut
    b. Had to be made
    c. To build houses
    d. Long and tedious work

34. What is the main problem in building the Nicaragua Canal?
    a. Many of the financial backers, like Ferdinand de Lesseps, are in jail
    b. The route needs to be cut through mountains
    c. The Nicaragua Canal is interrupting the treaty with Great Britain
    d. The canal route goes past a volcano

35. Why does the author discuss the Panama Canal?
    a. He is highlighting the other great canal in Central America
    b. He is explaining the reasons why a canal is needed
    c. He is showing the first canal that was attempted and why it failed
    d. He is explaining how sailors avoid going around Cape Horn

36. Read this phrase from paragraph 19: *And when they lost it, it meant misery and poverty to them.* The author uses this sentence to show:
    a. The people who suffered the most from the failure to build the Panama Canal
    b. Why the Panama Canal failed
    c. Rich people suffered the most from the failure to build the Panama Canal
    d. The project of making a canal was not given up

37. The Nicaragua Canal will?
    a. Make sailing longer and more dangerous
    b. Help ships avoid Cape Horn
    c. Cause more people to take the train across the Isthmus of Panama
    d. Cut across the Isthmus at its very narrowest point

Questions 38 – 48 pertain to the following passages:

"The Ettrick Shepherd" by James Baldwin

Part I

(1) In Scotland there once lived a poor shepherd whose name was James Hogg. His father and grandfather and great-grandfather had all been shepherds.

(2) It was his business to take care of the sheep which belonged to a rich landholder by the Ettrick Water. Sometimes he had several hundreds of lambs to look after. He drove these to the pastures on the hills and watched them day after day while they fed on the short green grass.

- 40 -

(3) He had a dog which he called Sirrah. This dog helped him watch the sheep. He would drive them from place to place as his master wished. Sometimes he would take care of the whole flock while the shepherd was resting or eating his dinner.

(4) One dark night James Hogg was on the hilltop with a flock of seven hundred lambs. Sirrah was with him. Suddenly a storm came up. There was thunder and lightning; the wind blew hard; the rain poured.

(5) The poor lambs were frightened. The shepherd and his dog could not keep them together. Some of them ran towards the east, some towards the west, and some towards the south.

(6) The shepherd soon lost sight of them in the darkness. With his lighted lantern in his hand, he went up and down the rough hills calling for his lambs.

(7) Two or three other shepherds joined him in the search. All night long they sought for the lambs.

(8) Morning came and still they sought. They looked, as they thought, in every place where the lambs might have taken shelter.

(9) At last James Hogg said, "It's of no use; all we can do is to go home and tell the master that we have lost his whole flock."

(10) They had walked a mile or two towards home, when they came to the edge of a narrow and deep ravine. They looked down, and at the bottom they saw some lambs huddled together among the rocks. And there was Sirrah standing guard over them and looking all around for help. "These must be the lambs that rushed off towards the south," said James Hogg.

(11) The men hurried down and soon saw that the flock was a large one.

(12) "I really believe they are all here," said one.

(13) They counted them and were surprised to find that not one lamb of the great flock of seven hundred was missing.

(14) How had Sirrah managed to get the three scattered divisions together? How had he managed to drive all the frightened little animals into this place of safety?

(15) Nobody could answer these questions. But there was no shepherd in

Scotland that could have done better than Sirrah did that night.

(16) Long afterward James Hogg said, "I never felt so grateful to any creature below the sun as I did to Sirrah that morning."

Part II

(17) When James Hogg was a boy, his parents were too poor to send him to school. By some means, however, he learned to read; and after that he loved nothing so much as a good book.

(18) There were no libraries near him, and it was hard for him to get books. But he was anxious to learn. Whenever he could buy or borrow a volume of prose or verse he carried it with him until he had read it through. While watching his flocks, he spent much of his time in reading. He loved poetry and soon began to write poems of his own. These poems were read and admired by many people.

(19) The name of James Hogg became known all over Scotland. He was often called the Ettrick Shepherd, because he was the keeper of sheep near the Ettrick Water.

(20) Many of his poems are still read and loved by children as well as by grown up men and women. Here is one:

A Boy's Song

Where the pools are bright and deep,
Where the gray trout lies asleep,
Up the river and o'er the lea,
That's the way for Billy and me.
Where the blackbird sings the latest,
Where the hawthorn blooms the sweetest,
Where the nestlings chirp and flee,
That's the way for Billy and me.
Where the mowers mow the cleanest,
Where the hay lies thick and greenest,
There to trace the homeward bee,
That's the way for Billy and me.
Where the hazel bank is steepest,
Where the shadow falls the deepest,
Where the clustering nuts fall free,
That's the way for Billy and me.
Why the boys should drive away,
Little maidens from their play,
Or love to banter and fight so well,
That's the thing I never could tell.
But this I know, I love to play
In the meadow, among the hay—
Up the water, and o'er the lea,
That's the way for Billy and me.

38. Why is James Hogg called the Ettrick Shepherd?

    a. He lived in Scotland
    b. He kept sheep
    c. He lived near Ettrick Water
    d. He lived near Ettrick Water and kept sheep

39. Which of the following best describes the problem in paragraphs 1-16?

    a. The sheep ran away and James Hogg couldn't find them
    b. A storm came up and Sirrah got scared
    c. James Hogg had trouble of taking care of such a large flock
    d. James Hogg got lost in the darkness

40. What does the phrase, *Where the blackbird sings the latest*, from the poem "A Boy's Song" refer to?

    a. James and Billy's favorite type of bird
    b. A place where James and Billy like to play
    c. The hay
    d. James and Billy's favorite song

41. In paragraphs 11-16, how does James know all the sheep were in the ravine?

    a. Sirrah told him
    b. He counted the sheep
    c. He rounded them all up from the east, the west, and the south
    d. He was the best shepherd in Scotland

42. What does the poem show about the narrator's personality?

    a. He is playful
    b. He is afraid of shadows
    c. He is not curious
    d. He does not like to explore things

43. Use the story map to answer the question below.

Which of these belongs in the empty box on the story map?

    a. James wrote a poem about his sheep
    b. James searched for the flock
    c. James lived in Scotland
    d. Sirrah gathered up all of the sheep

44. Why did James Hogg take care of the sheep?

    a. He took care of them as a favor to the landholder
    b. He loved the lambs
    c. Taking care of the sheep was his job
    d. He liked spending time with Sirrah

45. In paragraph 18, the word *prose* means

    a. Book
    b. Writing
    c. Library
    d. To learn

46. What's the most important idea is expressed in "A Boy's Song"?

    a. Billy and the narrator are great friends
    b. Being a shepherd is hard work
    c. The narrator enjoys nature
    d. Billy and the narrator fight frequently

47. In paragraph 8, the word *sought* means?

    a. To see
    b. To think
    c. To seek
    d. to come

48. Which word best describes how James felt after he located the sheep?

    a. Surprised
    b. Scared
    c. Tired
    d. Disappointed

Answer Key and Explanations for Reading Test #1

TEKS Standard §110.20(b)(6)

1. C: The correct answer choice is C because paragraphs 2-5 introduce Buck and the setting in which he lives. The paragraphs accomplish this introduction by giving many detailed facts, such as the detail in paragraph 5 about the times he escorted Mollie and Alice on walks. Choice A is incorrect because two new characters, Manuel and the stranger, are introduced in paragraphs 7 and 8. While aspects of paragraphs 2-5 show Buck's personality, choice B is incorrect because the paragraphs also give other details about Buck, such as information about his parents and appearance. Choice D is incorrect because Toots and Ysabel are only mentioned in paragraphs 3 and 4. Furthermore, paragraph 4 says that he utterly ignored Toots and Ysabel, not that he is affectionate towards them.

TEKS Standard §110.20(b)(6)

2. B: The correct answer is choice B because the sentence indicates that Buck felt as if he owned or ruled over Judge Miller's place. The word *realm* indicates that the sentence is referring to everything. Choice A is incorrect because it talks about other dogs that came and went but does not show Buck's attitude towards them or Judge Miller's place. Choice C is incorrect because it shows Buck's opinion of himself but not his opinion of Judge Miller's place. Choice A is incorrect because it describes something that Buck enjoys, but does not give his attitude about the house and grounds at Judge Miller's.

TEKS Standard §110.20(b)(6)

3. B: The correct answer is choice B because details in the passage foreshadow what might happen to Buck. Phrases like "trouble was brewing" or "these men wanted dogs" indicate that one of the dogs men want or Buck might be heading for trouble. Choice A is incorrect because the paragraph does not give details about Buck's life; later paragraphs give those details. Choice C is incorrect because the paragraph does not give setting details. Setting details about Buck's current situation are given in later paragraphs. Choice D is incorrect because the paragraph does not describe any characters other than Buck; it does not indicate that Buck is the villain.

TEKS Standard §110.20(b)(6)

4. A: Choice A is the correct answer because the Klondike strike has caused people to look for dogs like Buck. Although paragraph 1 does not directly mention the Klondike strike, the reader can infer from paragraph 6 that the events discussed refer to the Klondike strike. Choice B is incorrect because paragraph 3 makes it clear that dogs came and went even before the Klondike strike. Choice C is incorrect because Elmo is Buck's father but not a main character in the story. Choice D is incorrect because the passage does not draw a connection between the Klondike strike and the frequency of the Raisin Growers' Association's meetings.

TEKS Standard §110.20(b)(2)(B)

5. D: Choice D is correct because the sentence indicates that Buck considers himself to be like a king. Kings or royalty are often considered regal. Choice A is incorrect because nothing in the paragraph indicates that Buck is scared; in fact, Buck is like a king, which makes him unlikely to be scared of the other dogs. Choice B is incorrect because Buck doesn't indicate anger, which could be shown by barking or growling. Choice C is incorrect because *regal* is referring to Buck feeling like a king, which is unrelated to his happiness.

TEKS Standard §110.20(b)(6)

6. C: Choice C is correct because the first part of the passage mostly describes Buck's life, but the passage ends in a moment of change when the stranger wraps a piece of rope around Buck's neck. Choice A is incorrect because the passage does not describe a sequence of events as they happen. Instead the passage gives an overview of how Buck lived before the moment of change. Although part of the passage describes Buck's history, the passage also describes the moment in which his life changes, making choice B incorrect. Choice D is incorrect because the passage only describes life at Judge Miller's place but doesn't describe what came afterwards.

TEKS Standard §110.20(b)(6)

7. A: The correct answer is choice A because most of the passage provides background information about Buck's life and personality. Choice B is incorrect because the passage does not describe any moments in which Buck is acting heroic; instead, it describes Buck's regular interactions with the other people and animals at Judge Miller's place. Choice C is incorrect because the passage only briefly mentions the Klondike strike. The majority of the passage describes Buck's life. Choice D is incorrect because the other dogs are described in paragraphs 3 and 4. The rest of the passage focuses on Buck.

TEKS Standard §110.20(b)(6)

8. C: The correct answer is choice C because the stranger ties a rope around Buck's neck. This action indicates that Buck will be forced to leave Judge Miller's place. Choice A is incorrect because the end of the passage indicates that Buck might be forced to leave Judge Miller's place, which means he won't be able to continue to act like a king. Choice B is incorrect because the passage does not mention Buck or Shep at the end; Buck's parents are only mentioned in paragraph 5 when the passage describes Buck's family background. Although Manuel is a gardener, choice D is incorrect because Buck is likely leaving the garden to go away with the stranger, which means he won't be able to spend more time in the garden.

TEKS Standard §110.20(b)(3)

9. A: The best answer is choice A because the passage begins by setting up Buck's life and then showing a moment where his life is about to drastically change. Choice B is incorrect because only paragraph 5 refers to family; this is not a big enough portion of the passage to imply that the larger selection is about family. Although Buck might need to work hard in the future, choice C is incorrect because the passage does not have that many clues about upcoming hard work. Choice C is incorrect because the passage does not spend time showing that Buck strongly values relationships. The end of the passage indicates that Buck is about to experience a moment of change.

TEKS Standard §110.20(b)(6)

10. B: The best answer is choice B because paragraph 2 describes Judge Miller's place in great detail, including a description of the house, the driveway, the stables, and the outhouses. Choice A is incorrect because the paragraph only says that his place is in the Santa Clara Valley; however, the paragraph does not describe the valley in detail (it only describes it as sun-kissed). Choice C is

- 46 -

incorrect because paragraphs 3 and 4 describe Buck's lifestyle, not paragraph 2. Choice D is incorrect because paragraph 2 does not mention the Klondike strike. The strike is referred to in paragraphs 1 and 6.

TEKS Standard §110.20(b)(6)

11. B: The correct answer is choice B because the sentence talks about how the men want dogs; the sentence foreshadows that Buck may be the type of dog that the men want. Choice A is incorrect because it refers to Buck's attitude around Judge Miller's place but does not hint at what might be coming next. Although part of the sentence indicates that Buck hopes to follow in Elmo's footsteps, the rest of the sentence simply describes Buck's father. Choice B better foreshadows what's going to happen in the story because it more closely relates to the events in paragraph 7 and 8. Choice D is incorrect because the sentence describes Buck's personality and interests without giving clues about what's going to happen next.

TEKS Standard §110.20(b)(6)

12. D: The best answer is choice D because, as a dog, Buck can't read. Although Buck may not be interested in current events, choice A is incorrect because choice D is a more logical answer. Choices B and C are also incorrect because the logic that Buck doesn't read the newspapers is drawn from the fact that dogs can't read.

TEKS Standard §110.20(b)(2)(B)

13. C: The correct answer is C because Andy and his family were in good spirits, or happy, when he left for school at the beginning of the term. Now that he's returned, he knows something is wrong, but isn't sure what it is. Choice A is incorrect because the passage does not discuss Andy's eye color. The phrase *different eyes* is used metaphorically and does not literally mean that Andy has different eyes. For this reason, choice B is also incorrect. Choice D is incorrect because Andy is uneasy rather than happy. He knows something bad has happened.

TEKS Standard §110.20(b)(8)

14. A: Choice A is the correct answer because the phrase *a heavy blow* refers to the very difficult situation that Andy's father now finds himself in. The difficult situation hit him like a hammer, or heavy blow, because it was sudden and very financially painful. While it's true that Andy can't go back to school, choice B is incorrect because the sentence refers to Andy's father rather than Andy. Although losing six thousand dollars is part of the heavy blow, choice C is incorrect because the sentence does not show how much money Andy's father lost. The reader finds out the amount of money in paragraph 11, while the sentence in the question does not appear until paragraph 14. Choice D is incorrect because the sentence does not refer to Andy.

TEKS Standard §110.20(b)(6)(A)

15. D: While parts of the other answer choices are correct, the best answer is choice D because it is the only choice that correctly summarizes the passage. Choice A is incorrect because Andy's father has not won six thousand dollars; he has lost that amount of money. Choice B is incorrect because Nathan Lawrence has stolen twenty thousand dollars, but only six thousand of that amount belonged to Andy's father. Choice C is incorrect because Andy is not cheerful that he doesn't have to go back to school; he likes school and is very disappointed.

16. B: The reader learns in paragraph 1 that Andy likes school. When Andy finds out he can't return to school, he is disappointed but he makes his voice sound cheerful when he's speaking to his family. Choice A is incorrect because it doesn't show Andy's feelings; it just shows that Andy knows how the family's misfortune will affect his studies. Choice C is incorrect because it simply contains Andy's new plans for the future and does not show his emotions. Choice D is incorrect even though this sentence does show Andy's emotions. However, this sentence refers to Andy's opinion about Squire Carter and not about returning to school.

TEKS Standard §110.20(b)(6)

17. D: Choice D is the correct answer. In paragraph 19, Frank says that he didn't agree to pay for both dinners, and then in paragraph 23 he asks for at least ten cents back. These two examples show that Frank thought Mr. Percy would return some of his money. Choice A is incorrect because Frank didn't intend to give all his money even though it may have been generous for Frank to buy Mr. Percy a drink. Choice B is incorrect because Mr. Percy didn't offer to pay for anything; in fact, he took money and didn't repay it. Choice C is incorrect because the passage does not indicate that Mr. Percy owes the money. Instead, it shows Mr. Percy tricking Frank in order to get Frank to buy him drinks.

TEKS Standard §110.20(b)(2)(B)

18. B: The correct answer is choice B because the word *capital* refers to money. The reader can use the context of the passage to find the meaning of *capital*. Frank lost his twenty-five cents, which means his capital had vanished. Even though *capital* refers to money, choice A is incorrect because Frank had twenty-five cents rather than just a penny. Choice C is incorrect because Mr. Percy is the one who calls Frank virtuous. Choice D is incorrect because it's not clear if Frank had a friendship with Mr. Percy in the first place. Therefore, his friendship would not have vanished.

TEKS Standard §110.20(b)(6)

19. C: Frank knew he did not have much money, but when he saw that he would get a free lunch if he bought a drink, he was willing to eat it. Even though Mr. Percy handed the bartender the money, choice A is incorrect because Mr. Percy handed over Frank's money. Choice B is incorrect because lunch was not completely free; he needed to buy a drink in order to get the free sandwiches. Choice D is incorrect because nothing in the passage indicates that Frank wanted to spend time with Mr. Percy. Instead, paragraph 8 says that Frank was hungry.

TEKS Standard §110.20(b)(6)

20. D: Choice D is the best answer because Mr. Percy used Frank's money in order to get the drinks. Even though Mr. Percy claims that he'll pay Frank tomorrow, the reader can infer that he is probably lying. Choice C is incorrect because Mr. Percy tells Frank to be virtuous and happy as a way of dismissing Frank. However, he does not withhold the money because he feels that Frank is undeserving. Choice A is incorrect because Mr. Percy ordered drinks that he could not pay for with his own money. Although Mr. Percy says he'll be in the park, choice B is incorrect because Mr. Percy might be lying.

TEKS Standard §110.20(b)(6)

21. A: Choice A is the correct answer because Frank has realized that he has just lost all his money. The word *ruefully* shows that Frank is disappointed. Choice B is incorrect because Frank acted incautiously earlier in the passage when he gave Mr. Percy all his money. By paragraph 25, Frank is no longer incautious. Choice C is incorrect because Frank feels uneasy in paragraph 23. By paragraph 25, Frank realizes that Mr. Percy has cheated him. Choice D is incorrect because Frank is no longer suspicious about Mr. Percy's actions; he already knows that Mr. Percy is not going to repay him.

TEKS Standard §110.20(b)(3) and (6)

22. B: The best answer is choice B because both Andy and Frank experience a form of misfortune. Andy's misfortune is that his family has lost money and he can't return to school. Frank's misfortune is that he is all alone in the city and does not have any money. Choice A is incorrect because only Andy has a loving family; paragraph 25 of *The Telegraph Boy* shows that Frank is all alone. Choice C is incorrect because only Frank was tricked. Andy's family lost money because a banker stole it from his father. Choice D is incorrect because only *The Telegraph Boy* shows that Frank experiences hunger. *Andy Grant's Pluck* does not indicate that Andy will have trouble buying food.

TEKS Standard §110.20(b)(6)

23. C: The correct answer is choice C because Andy has no control over his family's finances, while Frank's poor decision to trust Mr. Percy led to his misfortune. Although *The Telegraph Boy* does not explain how Frank ended up alone with only twenty-five cents, choice A is incorrect because *The Telegraph Boy* does show how he ended up with no money at all. Choice B is incorrect because Andy is not all alone (he has his family); similarly, Frank does not have many friends (he is all alone). Choice D is incorrect because Andy was not tricked; instead, his father was robbed.

TEKS Standard §110.20(b)(3) and (6)

24. D: The correct answer is D because both selections end after the main characters have suffered misfortune. They don't know what the future holds for them. Choice A is incorrect because the characters have only experienced bad things; they are not feeling hopeful. Choice B is incorrect because Andy in *Andy Grant's Pluck* can't afford to go back to school. Furthermore, Frank in *The Telegraph Boy* never mentions school. Choice C is incorrect because the characters are not in immediate danger; they are uncertain about their future, but there are no threatening things around them.

TEKS Standard §110.20(b)(6)

25. C: The correct answer is choice C because the sentence shows that Andy feels disappointed, or the opposite of cheerful. Frank also feels disappointed after he loses all his money. Choice A is incorrect because the sentence simply describes Andy's father's problem; it does not show feelings. Choice B is incorrect because it shows Andy's determination to help his father; *The Telegraph Boy* does not have any moments where Frank shows determination. Choice D is incorrect because it is stating a fact rather than a feeling.

TEKS Standard §110.20(b)(10)(A)

26. C: The correct answer is C because paragraph 2 says, "This new trouble concerns the building of the Nicaragua Canal." Choice A is incorrect because paragraph 5 says that people are looking for a way to avoid going around Cape Horn; sailors would be happy for a canal. Choice B is incorrect because the Panama Canal is an older, failed project. Paragraph D is incorrect because there is no canal called the Central America Canal. There are two possible canals that, if completed, would cut across Central America: the Nicaragua Canal and the Panama Canal.

TEKS Standard §110.20(b)(10)(A)

27. B: The correct answer choice is B because paragraphs 15-19 detail the many financial problems that hurt the Panama Canal project. These problems include the dishonesty of several people involved in building the canal. Even though paragraph 15 mentions the Suez Canal, choice A is incorrect because the paragraph only mentions the Suez Canal to explain who Ferdinand de Lesseps is. Paragraph 18 does mention the French newspapers, but choice C is incorrect because paragraphs 15-19 are mostly about the problems that hurt the Panama Canal. While the bribing of the newspapers was one of the problems, it wasn't the entire one. Choice D is incorrect because the paragraphs don't go into detail about Ferdinand de Lesseps' time in jail; they only mention that he went to jail.

TEKS Standard §110.20(b)(10)(A)

28. C: The correct answer is C because the sentence shows the dangers of going around Cape Horn. Choice A is incorrect because the sentence only discusses the way in which the Nicaragua Canal is affecting the treaty with Great Britain. Choice B is incorrect because it only details the location of Cape Horn without explaining why this location could encourage people to build a canal. Choice D is incorrect because it discusses steamships without explaining why a canal is needed.

TEKS Standard §110.20(b)(10)

29. A: The correct answer is A, informational, because the author includes many factual details about the Nicaragua and Panama Canals. Choice B is incorrect because the author strictly gives facts and does not include jokes that would make the passage humorous. Choice C is incorrect because the author doesn't withhold details that would add mystery to the passive. Choice D is incorrect because the author does not show emotions such as anger; he has an objective tone.

TEKS Standard §110.20(b)(10)(A)

30. D: The passage explains in paragraph 23 that the Nicaragua Canal will go through existing waterways, which means that the builders will not have to cut through much land. Choice A is incorrect because, even though the Nicaragua Canal is longer, only 21 of those miles need to be cut through. This number contrasts with the 59 miles of the Panama Canal that needed to be cut through. Choice B is incorrect because the Panama Canal needed to be cut through the mountains, not the Nicaragua Canal. Choice C is incorrect because the passage does not say that the San Juan River is a canal. It simply says in paragraph 23 that the Nicaragua Canal will go through the San Juan River.

TEKS Standard §110.20(b)(10)(A)

31. B: Although the passage does not give the date of the building of the Suez Canal, it does imply in paragraph 15 that the Suez Canal was built before the Panama and Nicaragua Canals when it says "the great Count Ferdinand de Lesseps, who built the Suez Canal." The passage also indicates that the Panama Canal was attempted before the Nicaragua Canal; the reason the Nicaragua Canal needed to be built was because the Panama Canal failed. Choices A, C, and D are incorrect because they do not show the correct chronological order.

TEKS Standard §110.20(b)(10)(A)

32. D: The correct answer is D because the author is discussing the new plans for a canal, which will be the Nicaragua Canal. The author does this by giving some background of canals in Central America and describing details of the Nicaragua Canal. Choices A and B are incorrect because the author is very objective and does not argue for or against the Nicaragua Canal project; instead, he just gives information. Although the author does explain the problems that ended the Panama Canal project (in paragraph 15-20), this description is a small portion of the passage. The main purpose is to describe the issues surrounding the Nicaragua Canal.

TEKS Standard §110.20(b)(2)(B)

33. A: The correct answer is A because blasting will create a long and deep cut in the in the earth. The first sentence of paragraph 22 says that a long and deep cut needed to be made. The next sentence says that this cut will be made by blasting. Choice B is incorrect because the phrase 'had to be made' doesn't give details about how blasting works. Choice C is incorrect because the phrase 'to build houses' talks about building something up rather than blasting something away. Choice D is incorrect because, while blasting may be long and tedious work, the phrase does not describe what blasting it is. It just describes the type of work that blasting is.

TEKS Standard §110.20(b)(10)(A)

34. D: Choice D is the correct answer because paragraph 24 says that there is a volcano in Nicaragua Lake, which the canal will go through. Choice A is incorrect because Ferdinand de Lesseps and the other people in jail backed the Panama Canal, not the Nicaragua Canal. Choice B is incorrect because paragraph 22 shows that the Panama Canal, not the Nicaragua Canal, went through the mountains. Although paragraphs 1 and 2 say that the treaty may be defeated or delayed, this treaty is not a problem in building the canal. In contrast, the building of the canal affects the treaty.

TEKS Standard §110.20(b)(10)(A)

35. C: The correct answer is C because the author wants to explain what happened in the past with the Panama Canal so readers can understand the history as well as possible problems with the Nicaragua Canal. Choice A is incorrect because the Panama Canal was never completed, which means it's not the other great canal in Central America. Choice B is incorrect because the author explains why the canal is needed in paragraphs 4-11. These paragraphs come before the discussion of the Panama Canal. Choice D is incorrect sailors still needed to go around Cape Horn because the Panama Canal was never completed. If the Nicaragua Canal is completed, the sailors will then be able to avoid Cape Horn.

TEKS Standard §110.20(b)(10)(A)

36. A: The correct answer is A because the sentence discusses the people who, according to the passage, were not rich, but lost money on the Panama Canal. These people suffered the most because they fell into deeper poverty. Choice B is incorrect because the sentence shows who suffered but does not show the problems that caused the money loss. Choice C is incorrect because paragraph 19 says that people who were not rich are the people who lost the money. Choice D is incorrect because paragraph 20 says that the canal failed and that the project was not completed.

TEKS Standard §110.20(b)(10)(A)

37. B: The correct answer is choice B because the passage explains that the only way for sailing vessels to get from the Atlantic Ocean to the Pacific Ocean is to go around Cape Horn. A canal will cut across Central America so that ships no longer need to go around Cape Horn. Choice A is incorrect because the canal will do the opposite by making sailing less dangerous. Choice C is incorrect because people needed to take the train before the canal was built. The train was the only way for people to go between shores while avoiding Cape Horn. Choice D is incorrect because the Panama Canal was planned to cut across at the narrowest point. The Nicaragua Canal would be 100 miles longer.

TEKS Standard §110.20(b)(7)

38. D: The correct answer is D because paragraph 19 says that he lived near Ettrick Water and that he was a keeper of sheep. Choice A is incorrect because he didn't get his nickname because he was Scottish; however, people all over Scotland knew who he was and called him the Ettrick Shepherd. Choices B and C are only partially correct. Both answers contributed to his nickname. Since choice D includes both, it is the best answer.

TEKS Standard §110.20(b)(7)

39. A: The passage says that the sheep scattered during the storm. James couldn't find them in the dark, although he did find them the next day. Choice B is incorrect because the passage does not say that Sirrah was scared; it says that the sheep were scared. Choice C is incorrect because paragraph 2 says that James sometimes watched several hundred sheep; he only had a problem with so many sheep when they became scared by the storm. Choice D is incorrect because the passage doesn't say that James got lost; instead, paragraph 6 says that he *lost sight* of the sheep. He knew where he was, but couldn't find the sheep.

TEKS Standard §110.20(b)(4)

40. B: The best answer is choice B because the poem describes several of the narrator's favorite places. The key word from the phrase is 'where'. The phrase is describing a specific place. Choice A is incorrect because the poem does not indicate that the narrator and Billy prefer blackbirds to other birds. Choice C is incorrect because the phrase "Where the blackbird sings the latest" is referring to the meadow. The next verse discusses the hay. Choice D is incorrect because the narrator doesn't say that the blackbird's song is his favorite song; he just mentions the song.

TEKS Standard §110.20(b)(7)

41. B: Choice B is correct because paragraph 13 says that James and the other shepherds counted the sheep to determine that they were all there. Choice A is incorrect because Sirrah is a dog and cannot speak. Choice C is incorrect because Sirrah rounded up the sheep, not James. Choice D is incorrect because the passage does not say he was the best shepherd; in fact, the passage does not describe the quality of his skills at all.

TEKS Standard §110.20(b)(4)

42. A: The correct answer is A because the poem shows a sense of wonder and excitement. The last verse also says, "I love to play", which shows how much the narrator likes to play and have fun. Choice B is incorrect because the narrator does not show fear. Instead, he shows an enthusiasm for life. Choice C is incorrect because the poem shows a lot of curiosity; the narrator describes all his favorite places and may be curious about them. Choice D is incorrect because the narrator demonstrates his love of exploring when he describes all the details of the meadow, the hay, the water, and the lea.

TEKS Standard §110.20(b)(7)

43. B: The correct answer is B because paragraph 6 says that James started searching for the sheep once he realized they were gone. Choice A is incorrect because the selection does not indicate that James wrote a poem immediately after losing the sheep. Furthermore, the poem in the passage is not about the sheep. Choice C is incorrect because James always lived in Scotland; the answer choice is not an event that happened after he lost the sheep. While it's true that Sirrah gathered up the sheep, choice D is incorrect because it happened after James searched for the sheep.

TEKS Standard §110.20(b)(7)

44. C: The correct answer is choice C because paragraph 2 says that it was his business to take care of the sheep, which means that it was his job. Choice A is incorrect because the passage shows that being a shepherd is his business. He makes money from doing it, which means he's not doing a favor. Choice B is incorrect for the same reason; James may like the sheep, but he takes care of them to earn money. Choice D is also incorrect; while James liked Sirrah and says in paragraph 16 that he is grateful to him, James is a shepherd because it's his family's business.

TEKS Standard §110.20(b)(2)(B)

45. B: The correct answer is B. The passage says that he read through the prose, which implies that the prose is a form of writing. While the prose is in a book, choice A is incorrect because the word 'volume' is referring to the book. Choice C is incorrect because the paragraph says that no libraries were near James Hogg. When he wanted a book of prose, he needed to buy or borrow it. Choice D is incorrect because he may have learned from the book, but 'prose' does not mean to learn. It is a noun that means a type of writing.

TEKS Standard §110.20(b)(4)

46. A: The correct answer is A because the narrator frequently mentions doing things with Billy. The phrase "That's the way for Billy and me" shows that the narrator and Billy probably spend a lot of time together and are friends. Choice B is incorrect because the poem does not refer to being a shepherd at all. While the poem expresses the narrator's loves nature, the repeated mention of Billy at the end of each verse emphasizes the close friendship between the narrator and Billy. Choice D is incorrect because the poem indicates that Billy and the narrator are friends. Although the third verse mentions fighting, it does not refer to fighting with Billy.

TEKS Standard §110.20(b)(2)(B)

47. C: It is clear from paragraph 7 that James and the other shepherds are looking for the sheep. The second sentence of paragraph 8 also shows that they are looking for the sheep. Choice A is incorrect because 'sought' means to look for something, not to see something, as shown in

- 53 -

paragraphs 7 and 8. While the word *sought* rhymes with *thought*, it means to seek or look for something, as indicated by the second sentence of the paragraph. Choice D is incorrect because James and the shepherds are looking for the sheep.

TEKS Standard §110.20(b)(7)

48. A: James felt surprised because Sirrah managed to gather all the sheep; the selection says he's surprised in paragraph 13. Choice B is incorrect because, while James might have been scared during the storm, he was relieved when he found the sheep. While James might have felt tired after staying up all night, choice A is a better answer than choice C because the passage says that he and the shepherds were surprised. Choice D is incorrect because James had no reason to be disappointed; he found the sheep he thought he had lost and was happy.

Reading Practice Test #2

Questions 1 – 12 pertain to the following passage:

"The Cruel Crane Outwitted" from Indian Fairy Tales

(1) Long ago the Bodisat was born to a forest life as the Genius of a tree standing near a certain lotus pond.

(2) Now at that time the water used to run short at the dry season in a certain pond, not over large, in which there were a good many fish. And a crane thought on seeing the fish.

(3) "I must outwit these fish somehow or other and make a prey of them."

(4) And he went and sat down at the edge of the water, thinking how he should do it.

(5) When the fish saw him, they asked him, "What are you sitting there for, lost in thought?"

(6) "I am sitting thinking about you," said he.

(7) "Oh, sir! what are you thinking about us?" said they.

(8) "Why," he replied; "there is very little water in this pond, and but little for you to eat; and the heat is so great! So I was thinking, 'What in the world will these fish do now?'"

(9) "Yes, indeed, sir! what *are* we to do?" said they.

(10) "If you will only do as I bid you, I will take you in my beak to a fine large pond, covered with all the kinds of lotuses, and put you into it," answered the crane.

(11) "That a crane should take thought for the fishes is a thing unheard of, sir, since the world began. It's eating us, one after the other, that you're aiming at."

(12) "Not I! So long as you trust me, I won't eat you. But if you don't believe me that there is such a pond, send one of you with me to go and see it."

(13) Then they trusted him, and handed over to him one of their number—a big fellow, blind of one eye, whom they thought sharp enough in any emergency, afloat or ashore.

(14) Him the crane took with him, let him go in the pond, showed him the whole of it, brought him back, and let him go again close to the other fish. And he told them all the glories of the pond.

(15) And when they heard what he said, they exclaimed, "All right, sir! You may take us with you."

(16) Then the crane took the old purblind fish first to the bank of the other pond, and alighted in a Varana-tree growing on the bank there. But he threw it into a fork of the tree, struck it with his beak, and killed it; and then ate its flesh, and threw its bones away at the foot of the tree. Then he went back and called out:

(17) "I've thrown that fish in; let another one come."

(18) And in that manner he took all the fish, one by one, and ate them, till he came back and found no more!

(19) But there was still a crab left behind there; and the crane thought he would eat him too, and called out:

(20) "I say, good crab, I've taken all the fish away, and put them into a fine large pond. Come along. I'll take you too!"

(21) "But how will you take hold of me to carry me along?"

(22) "I'll bite hold of you with my beak."

(23) "You'll let me fall if you carry me like that. I won't go with you!"

(24) "Don't be afraid! I'll hold you quite tight all the way."

(25) Then said the crab to himself, "If this fellow once got hold of fish, he would never let them go in a pond! Now if he should really put me into the pond, it would be capital; but if he doesn't—then I'll cut his throat, and kill him!" So he said to him:

(26) "Look here, friend, you won't be able to hold me tight enough; but we crabs have a famous grip. If you let me catch hold of you round the neck with my claws, I shall be glad to go with you."

(27) And the other did not see that he was trying to outwit him, and agreed. So the crab caught hold of his neck with his claws as securely as with a pair of blacksmith's pincers, and called out, "Off with you, now!"

(28) And the crane took him and showed him the pond, and then turned off towards the Varana-tree.

(29) "Uncle!" cried the crab, "the pond lies that way, but you are taking me this way!"

(30) "Oh, that's it, is it?" answered the crane. "Your dear little uncle, your very sweet nephew, you call me! You mean me to understand, I suppose, that I am your slave, who has to lift you up and carry you about with him! Now cast your eye upon the heap of fish-bones lying at the root of yonder Varana-tree. Just as I have eaten those fish, every one of them, just so I will devour you as well!"

(31) "Ah! those fishes got eaten through their own stupidity," answered the crab; "but I'm not going to let you eat *me*. On the contrary, is it *you* that I am going to destroy. For you in your folly have not seen that I was outwitting you. If we die, we die both together; for I will cut off this head of yours, and cast it to the ground!" And so saying, he gave the crane's neck a grip with his claws, as with a vice.

(32) Then gasping, and with tears trickling from his eyes, and trembling with the fear of death, the crane beseeched him, saying, "O my Lord! Indeed I did not intend to eat you. Grant me my life!"

(33) "Well, well! step down into the pond, and put me in there."

(34) And he turned round and stepped down into the pond, and placed the crab on the mud at its edge. But the crab cut through its neck as clean as one would cut a lotus-stalk with a hunting-knife, and then only entered the water!

(35) When the Genius who lived in the Varana-tree saw this strange affair, he made the wood resound with his plaudits, uttering in a pleasant voice the verse:

(36) "The villain, though exceeding clever,

Shall prosper not by his villainy.

He may win indeed, sharp-witted in deceit,

But only as the Crane here from the Crab!"

1. In paragraph 26, why does the crab makes plans to defend himself?
    a. He's worried that he'll fall
    b. He's worried the crane won't really take him to the pond
    c. He's friends with the crane
    d. He's glad to go with the crane

2. Why are the fish skeptical of the crane?
    a. The crane likes to help out fish
    b. The crane is making the pond run dry
    c. The crane likes to eat fish
    d. They might fall out of the crane's beak

3. The context of paragraphs 13-16, helps the reader know that *purblind* most likely means:
    a. Blind in one eye
    b. Blind in two eyes
    c. Old
    d. Trustworthy

4. Why did the crane agree to bring the crab to the pond?
    a. Because he always kept his word
    b. Because the crab asked him to
    c. Because the Genius told him to
    d. Because the crab threatened him

5. The author organizes the story mainly by:
    a. introducing Bodisat and showing his role in the crane's story
    b. using cause and effect to show what happens when a pond runs dry
    c. telling a story and then giving a moral
    d. giving a moral and then telling a story that supports it

6. Which of these is the best summary of the selection?

a. The pond that the fish live in is drying up, and the crane offers to take the fish to a pond with more water. The fish don't trust the crane, so they send a representative to check out the new pond. He says that the pond exists, so they all agree to go with the crane. The crane drops them off at the pond and then comes back to take the crab. The crab also doesn't trust the crane, but the crane is honest and also takes him to the pond.

b. The pond that the fish live in is drying up, and the crane offers to take the fish to a pond with more water. The fish don't trust the crane, so they send a representative to check out the new pond. He says that the pond exists, so they all agree to go with the crane. Instead of taking the fish to the pond, the crane eats each one. He then goes back to the dry pond and offers to take the crab. The crab also doesn't trust the crane, but the crane is honest this time and takes him straight to the new pond.

c. The pond that the fish live in is drying up, and the crane offers to take the fish to a pond with more water. The fish don't trust the crane, so they send a representative to check out the new pond. He says that the pond exists, so they all agree to go with the crane. Instead of taking the fish to the pond, the crane eats each one. He then goes back to the dry pond and offers to take the crab. The crab also doesn't trust the crane, so he creates a plan to force the crane to take him to the pond. Just when the crane is about to eat the crab, the crab attacks him. The crane quickly eats him up.

d. The pond that the fish live in is drying up, and the crane offers to take the fish to a pond with more water. The fish don't trust the crane, so they send a representative to check out the new pond. He says that the pond exists, so they all agree to go with the crane. Instead of taking the fish to the pond, the crane eats each one. He then goes back to the dry pond and offers to take the crab. The crab also doesn't trust the crane, so he creates a plan to force the crane to take him to the pond. When the crane tries to veer away from the pond to eat the crab, the crab attacks him. The crane agrees to take the crab to the pond. When they get to the pond, the crab attacks the crane again.

7. The author mentions Bodisat at the beginning and end of the story in order to show that

a. Bodisat is the main character of the story
b. the story is non-fiction
c. the story is a fable
d. the story is realistic fiction

8. In paragraph 6, what does the crane mean when he says, "I am sitting thinking about you."?

a. That he's worried about the fish
b. That he's worried about the crab
c. That he's thinking of a way to trick the fish
d. That he's thinking about the larger pond

9. How are the crane and the crab similar?

a. They both live in water
b. They both like to eat fish
c. They are both deceitful
d. They both enjoy each other's company

10. In paragraph 30, what proof does the crane present?
    a. The new pond is larger than the old pond
    b. He ate the fish
    c. He ate the crab
    d. The fish are stupid

11. What is the moral of this story?
    a. Villains succeed by being especially evil
    b. Villains succeed by tricking others
    c. Villains that are exceedingly clever are evil
    d. Villains prosper by their villainy

12. In paragraph 27, what does the phrase "blacksmith's pincers" show about the crab?
    a. That his claws close tightly
    b. That his claws are sharp
    c. That he wants to hurt the crane
    d. That he's excited to go to the pond

Questions 13 – 16 pertain to the following passage:

"Five Children and It" by E. Nesbit

(1) The house was three miles from the station, but, before the dusty hired hack had rattled along for five minutes, the children began to put their heads out of the carriage window and say, "Aren't we nearly there?" And every time they passed a house, which was not very often, they all said, "Oh, *is* this it?" But it never was, till they reached the very top of the hill, just past the chalk-quarry and before you come to the gravel-pit. And then there was a white house with a green garden and an orchard beyond, and mother said, "Here we are!"

(2) "How white the house is," said Robert.

(3) "And look at the roses," said Anthea.

(4) "And the plums," said Jane.

(5) "It is rather decent," Cyril admitted.

(6) The Baby said, "Wanty go walky;" and the hack stopped with a last rattle and jolt.

(7) Everyone got its legs kicked or its feet trodden on in the scramble to get out of the carriage that very minute, but no one seemed to mind. Mother, curiously enough, was in no hurry to get out; and even when she had come down slowly and by the step, and with no jump at all, she seemed to wish to see the boxes carried in, and even to pay the driver, instead of joining in that first glorious rush round the garden and orchard and the thorny, thistly, briery, brambly wilderness beyond the broken gate and the dry fountain at the side of the house. But the children were wiser, for once. It was not really a pretty house at all; it was quite ordinary, and mother thought it was rather inconvenient, and was quite annoyed at there being no shelves, to speak of, and hardly a cupboard in the place. Father used to say that the iron-work on the roof and coping was like an architect's nightmare. But the house was deep in the country, with no other house in sight, and the children had been in London for two years, without so much as once going to the seaside even for a day by an excursion

- 59 -

train, and so the White House seemed to them a sort of Fairy Palace set down in an Earthly Paradise. For London is like prison for children, especially if their relations are not rich.

13. Read the sentence from paragraph 7:

But the children were wiser for once.

What are the children wise about?
   a. They know that the house is nicer than it looks
   b. They know the house is less nice than it looked at first glance
   c. They know that being at a house in the country will be better than being in London
   d. They know that the broken-down house will convince Mother to take them back to London

14. What phrase from the passage best shows the children's emotions when they arrive at the house?
   a. And then there was a white house with a green garden and an orchard beyond
   b. How white the house is
   c. Everyone got its legs kicked or its feet trodden on in the scramble to get out of the carriage
   d. It was not really a pretty house

15. Which of these best describes the selection?
   a. The children are moving into a new house in London after living in the country
   b. The children are moving into a new house in the country after living in London
   c. The children are moving to a house in a new country
   d. The children are moving from a prison to a fairy palace

16. What's the most logical reason why Mother was not in a hurry to get out of the carriage?
   a. She's unhappy to be moving into the new house
   b. She's excited to see the new house
   c. She does not want to explore with children
   d. She needs to help the driver

Questions 17 -21 pertain to the following passage:

"The Railway Children" by E. Nesbit

(1) "Wake up, dears. We're there."

(2) They woke up, cold and melancholy, and stood shivering on the draughty platform while the baggage was taken out of the train. Then the engine, puffing and blowing, set to work again, and dragged the train away. The children watched the tail-lights of the guard's van disappear into the darkness.

(3) This was the first train the children saw on that railway which was in time to become so very dear to them. They did not guess then how they would grow to love the railway, and how soon it would become the centre of their new life, nor what wonders and changes it would bring to them. They only shivered and sneezed and hoped the walk to the new house would not be long. Peter's nose was colder than he ever remembered it to have been before. Roberta's hat was crooked, and the elastic seemed tighter than usual. Phyllis's shoe-laces had come undone.

(4) "Come," said Mother, "we've got to walk. There aren't any cabs here."

- 60 -

(5) The walk was dark and muddy. The children stumbled a little on the rough road, and once Phyllis absently fell into a puddle, and was picked up damp and unhappy. There were no gas-lamps on the road, and the road was uphill. The cart went at a foot's pace, and they followed the gritty crunch of its wheels. As their eyes got used to the darkness, they could see the mound of boxes swaying dimly in front of them.

(6) A long gate had to be opened for the cart to pass through, and after that the road seemed to go across fields—and now it went down hill. Presently a great dark lumpish thing showed over to the right.

(7) "There's the house," said Mother. "I wonder why she's shut the shutters."

(8) "Who's SHE?" asked Roberta.

(9) "The woman I engaged to clean the place, and put the furniture straight and get supper."

(10) There was a low wall, and trees inside.

(11) "That's the garden," said Mother.

(12 "It looks more like a dripping-pan full of black cabbages," said Peter.

(13) The cart went on along by the garden wall, and round to the back of the house, and here it clattered into a cobble-stoned yard and stopped at the back door.

(14) There was no light in any of the windows.

(15) Everyone hammered at the door, but no one came.

(16) The man who drove the cart said he expected Mrs.Viney had gone home.

(17) "You see your train was that late," said he.

(18) "But she's got the key," said Mother. "What are we to do?"

(19) "Oh, she'll have left that under the doorstep," said the cart man; "folks do hereabouts." He took the lantern off his cart and stooped.

(20) "Ay, here it is, right enough," he said.

(21) He unlocked the door and went in and set his lantern on the table.

(22) "Got e'er a candle?" said he.

(23) "I don't know where anything is." Mother spoke rather less cheerfully than usual.

(24) He struck a match. There was a candle on the table, and he lighted it. By its thin little glimmer the children saw a large bare kitchen with a stone floor. There were no curtains, no hearth-rug. The kitchen table from home stood in the middle of the room. The chairs were in one corner, and the pots, pans, brooms, and crockery in another. There was no fire, and the black grate showed cold, dead ashes.

(25) As the cart man turned to go out after he had brought in the boxes, there was a rustling, scampering sound that seemed to come from inside the walls of the house.

(26) "Oh, what's that?" cried the girls.

(27) "It's only the rats," said the cart man. And he went away and shut the door, and the sudden draught of it blew out the candle.

(28) "Oh, dear," said Phyllis, "I wish we hadn't come!" and she knocked a chair over.

(29) "ONLY the rats!" said Peter, in the dark.

17. Which of these is NOT a reason why the walk to the house was difficult?
    a. The road was muddy
    b. There was not any light along the road
    c. The walk was long
    d. The road was not smooth

18. In paragraph 15, why did no one come to the door?
    a. Mrs. Viney was running an errand
    b. The train was late
    c. Mrs. Viney didn't hear the knocking
    d. The door was unlocked

19. Which state below best reflects the impression made in paragraph 24?
    a. The house is homey and cozy
    b. The house is not homey or cozy
    c. Mrs. Viney lit a fire to welcome the family
    d. The house is missing furniture

20. What can the reader conclude about the passage?
    a. The children are excited to arrive at the house
    b. The children love the train and railroad
    c. The family is friends with Mrs. Viney
    d. The children are seeing the house for the first time

21. Which sentence or phrase from the passage best illustrates why the author chose the story's title?
    a. The baggage was taken out of the train
    b. Then the engine, puffing and blowing
    c. The children watched the tail-lights of the guard's van disappear into the darkness
    d. Which in time was to become so very dear to them

Questions 22 – 25 pertain to both passages from "Five Children and It" and "The Railway Children"

22. What do the children in "Five Children and It" have in common with the children in "The Railway Children"?
    a. They are excited to move into their new house
    b. They are moving to an unfamiliar location
    c. They are disappointed when they see their new house
    d. They are eager to explore the country

23. Which sentence or phrase from "Five Children and It" shows that the mothers in both stories felt the same about the new house?

    a. The house was three miles from the station
    b. Mother said, "Here we are!"
    c. Mother, curiously enough, was in no hurry to get out
    d. But the house was deep in the country

24. What's the difference in the way the children in the two stories perceive their new houses?

    a. The children in "Five Children and It" feel like their new house is a prison, but the children in "The Railway Children" are excited to explore
    b. The children in "Five Children and It" feel like their new house is a prison, and the children in "The Railway Children" think their new house is run down
    c. The children in "Five Children and It" are disappointed that their new house seems run-down, but the children in "The Railway Children" think their new house is a wonderful as a fairy palace
    d. The children in "Five Children and It" think their new house is wonderful even though it's run down, but the children in "The Railway Children" are not excited about moving into a rundown house

25. Both passages are the beginning of longer works. What do these beginnings have in common?

    a. They place the characters in a new setting
    b. They place the characters in an uncomfortable situation
    c. They introduce the characters by describing their appearance and personality
    d. They foreshadow that the children in both stories will argue with their parents

Questions 26 – 37 pertain to the following passage:

A Child's History of England by Charles Dickens

(1) If you look at a Map of the World, you will see, in the left-hand upper corner of the Eastern Hemisphere, two Islands lying in the sea. They are England and Scotland, and Ireland. England and Scotland form the greater part of these Islands. Ireland is the next in size. The little neighbouring islands, which are so small upon the Map as to be mere dots, are chiefly little bits of Scotland,—broken off, I dare say, in the course of a great length of time, by the power of the restless water.

(2) In the old days, a long, long while ago..., these Islands were in the same place, and the stormy sea roared round them, just as it roars now. But the sea was not alive, then, with great ships and brave sailors, sailing to and from all parts of the world. It was very lonely. The Islands lay solitary, in the great expanse of water. The foaming waves dashed against their cliffs, and the bleak winds blew over their forests; but the winds and waves brought no adventurers to land upon the Islands, and the savage Islanders knew nothing of the rest of the world, and the rest of the world knew nothing of them.

(3) It is supposed that the Phoenicians, who were an ancient people, famous for carrying on trade, came in ships to these Islands, and found that they produced tin and lead; both very useful things, as you know, and both produced to this very hour upon the sea-coast. The most celebrated tin mines in Cornwall are, still, close to the sea. One of them, which I have seen, is so close to it that it is hollowed out underneath the ocean; and the miners say, that in stormy weather, when they are at work down in that deep place, they can hear the noise of the waves thundering above their heads. So, the Phœnicians, coasting about the Islands, would come, without much difficulty, to where the tin and lead were.

- 63 -

(4) The Phœnicians traded with the Islanders for these metals, and gave the Islanders some other useful things in exchange. The Islanders were, at first, poor savages, going almost naked, or only dressed in the rough skins of beasts, and staining their bodies, as other savages do, with coloured earths and the juices of plants. But the Phœnicians, sailing over to the opposite coasts of France and Belgium, and saying to the people there, 'We have been to those white cliffs across the water, which you can see in fine weather, and from that country, which is called Britain, we bring this tin and lead,' tempted some of the French and Belgians to come over also. These people settled themselves on the south coast of England, which is now called Kent; and, although they were a rough people too, they taught the savage Britons some useful arts, and improved that part of the Islands. It is probable that other people came over from Spain to Ireland, and settled there.

(5) Thus, by little and little, strangers became mixed with the Islanders, and the savage Britons grew into a wild, bold people; almost savage, still, especially in the interior of the country away from the sea where the foreign settlers seldom went; but hardy, brave, and strong.

(6) The whole country was covered with forests, and swamps. The greater part of it was very misty and cold. There were no roads, no bridges, no streets, no houses that you would think deserving of the name. A town was nothing but a collection of straw-covered huts, hidden in a thick wood, with a ditch all round, and a low wall, made of mud, or the trunks of trees placed one upon another. The people planted little or no corn, but lived upon the flesh of their flocks and cattle. They made no coins, but used metal rings for money. They were clever in basket-work, as savage people often are; and they could make a coarse kind of cloth, and some very bad earthenware. But in building fortresses they were much more clever.

(7) They made boats of basket-work, covered with the skins of animals, but seldom, if ever, ventured far from the shore. They made swords, of copper mixed with tin; but, these swords were of an awkward shape, and so soft that a heavy blow would bend one. They made light shields, short pointed daggers, and spears—which they jerked back after they had thrown them at an enemy, by a long strip of leather fastened to the stem. The butt-end was a rattle, to frighten an enemy's horse. The ancient Britons, being divided into as many as thirty or forty tribes, each commanded by its own little king, were constantly fighting with one another, as savage people usually do; and they always fought with these weapons.

26. According to the author, why did the ancient Britons frequently fight with each other?

   a. They had many weapons
   b. They disliked the Phoenicians
   c. There were no roads or bridges
   d. They were divided into many tribes

27. What is paragraph 2 mostly about?

   a. The Map of the World
   b. The two islands and what they looked like
   c. The two islands and the people who lived there
   d. The winds and waves that blew against the island

28. Which sentence or phrase best shows the impact the Phoenicians had on the ancient Britons?

   a. The Phoenicians traded with the Islanders
   b. But the Phoenicians, sailing over to the opposite coasts of France and Belgium
   c. These people settled themselves on the south Coast of England
   d. The savage Britons grew into a wild, bold people

29. The tone throughout the selection is

   a. humorous
   b. informative
   c. angry
   d. bored

30. Which sentence or phrase best expresses the isolation of the islands of England and Scotland and Ireland?

   a. Which are so small upon the Map as to be mere dots
   b. The Islands lay solitary, in the great expanse of water
   c. They can hear the noise of the waves thundering above their heads
   d. Thus, by little and little, strangers became mixed with the Islanders

31. This passage is part of a longer work. Where does this selection most likely fit into the longer work?

   a. The beginning of the entire work
   b. The middle of a chapter
   c. The end of a chapter
   d. The end of the entire work

32. Read this phrase from paragraph 7:

   But seldom, if ever, ventured far from the shore.

Why does the author include this phrase?

   a. To show the ways in which the people used boats
   b. To highlight the irony of making boats
   c. To show where the people used weapons
   d. To explain why the people built fortresses

33. What most likely tempted the French and Belgians to come over to Britain?

   a. The white cliffs of Britain
   b. The fine weather
   c. The tin and lead
   d. Juices of plants

34. This passage is mostly likely to appear in a:

   a. Newspaper
   b. Travel book
   c. Textbook
   d. Novel

35. Look at the time line below:

1. The Phoenicians began trading with the ancient Britons

2. French and Belgian people moved to England

3. The Phoenicians discovered tin and lead on the coast

Which answer choice shows the correct order of events?
    a. No change
    b. 1, 3, 2
    c. 2, 1 3
    d. 3, 1, 2

36. Why does the author begin the passage by describing a map?
    a. To explain the location of the islands
    b. To show the roads that run through England, Scotland, and Ireland
    c. To show how the little bits of Scotland broke away from the main island
    d. To show the size of the islands in relation to France and Belgium

37. What sentence or phrase best describes the lands in the interior of the islands (the parts away from the coast)?
    a. These people settled themselves on the south coast of England, which is now called Kent
    b. Especially in the interior of the country away from the sea where the foreign settlers seldom went
    c. The whole country was covered with forests and swamps.
    d. The ancient Britons, being divided into as many as thirty or forty tribes, each commanded by its own king

Questions 38 – 48 pertain to the following passage:

Ten Boys from Dickens

"The Boy Musician"

By Kate Dickinson Sweetser

(1) Johannes Chrysostemus Wolfgangus Theophilus Mozart—what a burden to be put upon a baby's tiny shoulders!

(2) If there is any truth underlying the belief that a name can in some measure foreshadow a child's future, then surely Wolfgang Mozart, who was born in Salzburg in 1756, came honestly by his heritage of greatness, for when he was only a day old he received the five-part name, to which was later added his confirmation name of Sigismundus. But as soon as

- 66 -

he could choose for himself, the little son of Marianne and Leopold Mozart from his store of names, selected Wolfgang, to which he added Amadeus, by which combination he was always known, and the name is for ever linked with the memory of a great genius.

(3) Almost before he could talk plainly the little fellow showed himself to be a musical prodigy, and when he was scarcely three years old he would steal into the room where his father was giving a lesson on the harpsichord to Anna (or "Nannerl," as she was called), the sister five years older than himself, and while she was being taught, Wolfgang would listen and watch with breathless attention.

(4) One day when the lesson was over, he begged his father to teach him too, but Leopold Mozart only laughed as he answered, glancing down into the child's serious face looking so intently into his:

(5) "Wait, my little man, thou art but a baby yet. Wait awhile, my Wolferl!" and the disappointed little musician crept away, but as soon as Nannerl and his father had left the room, the tiny fellow crept back again, went to the harpsichord and standing on tiptoe, touched the keys with his chubby fingers stretched wide apart until he reached and played *a perfect chord*! Leopold Mozart was in another part of the house, but his sensitive ear caught the sound, and he rushed back to find his baby on tiptoe before the harpsichord, giving the first hint of his marvellous ability.

(6) At once the proud and excited father began to give him lessons, and always, too, from that day, whenever Nannerl had her lesson, Wolfgang perched on his father's knee, and listened with rapt absorption, and often when the lesson was over, he would repeat what she had played in exact imitation of her manner of playing.

(7) Leopold Mozart, who was himself a talented musician, saw with pride almost beyond expression, that both of his children inherited his musical ability, and soon felt that Wolfgang was a genius. When the boy was only four, his father, to test his powers, tried to teach him some minuets which to his perfect astonishment, Wolfgang played after him in a most extraordinary manner, not merely striking the notes correctly, but marking the rhythm with accurate expression, and to learn and play each minuet the little fellow required only half an hour.

(8) When he was five years old, one day his father entered the sitting-room of their home and found Wolfgang bending over a table, writing so busily that he did not hear his father enter, or see that he was standing beside him. Wolfgang's chubby little hand held the pen awkwardly, but held it with firm determination while it travelled back and forth across a large sheet of paper on which he was scribbling a strange collection of hieroglyphics, with here and there a huge blot, testifying to his haste and inexperience in the use of ink.

(9) What was he trying to do? His father's curiosity finally overcame him and he asked:

(10) "What are you doing, Wolfgang?" The curly head was raised with an impatient gesture.

(11) "I am composing a concerto for the harpsichord. I have nearly finished the first part."

(12) "Let me see it."

(13) "No, please, I have not yet finished."

(14) But even as he spoke, the eager father had taken up the paper and carried it over to where a friend stood, and they looked it over together, exchanging amused glances at the queer characters on it. Presently Leopold Mozart, after looking carefully at it, said:

(15) "Why it really seems to be composed by rule! But it is so difficult that no one could ever play it."

(16) "Oh, yes, they could, but it must be studied first," exclaimed little Wolfgang eagerly, and running to the harpsichord, he added:

(17) "See, this is the way it begins," and he was able to play enough of it, to show what his idea in writing it had been, and his father and the friend who had before exchanged glances of amusement, now looked at each other with wonder not untouched with awe.

38. Why does Leopold Mozart refuse to teach Wolfgang how to play the harpsichord at first?

   a. He does not think Wolfgang has talent
   b. Wolfgang has already shown he is a musical genius
   c. He thinks Wolfgang is too young
   d. He only wanted Anna to learn harpsichord

39. This passage describes real people from history. Which aspect of the passage is most likely made up by the author?

   a. The names of Wolfgang and his family members
   b. The dialogue between Wolfgang and Leopold
   c. The age at which Wolfgang composed the concerto
   d. The speed with which Wolfgang learned to play minuets

40. Which sentence or phrase from the passage best helps the reader infer that Wolferl is a nickname for Wolfgang?

   a. Johannes Chrysostemus Wolfgangus Theophilus Mozart – what a burden to be put upon a baby's tiny shoulders!
   b. But as soon as he could choose for himself, the little son of Marianne and Leopold Mozart from his store of names, selected Wolfgang, to which he added Amadeus
   c. He would steal into the room where his father was giving a lesson on the harpsichord to Anna (or "Nannerl," as she was called), the sister five years older than himself
   d. "Wait, my little man, thou art but a baby yet."

41. In paragraph 5, Leopold says he does not want to teach Wolfgang harpsichord yet. What makes him change his mind?

   a. Anna asks him
   b. Wolfgang asks him
   c. Wolfgang plays a chord by himself
   d. Wolfgang composes a concerto

42. In paragraph 8, the phrase "a strange collection of hieroglyphics" most likely refers to

   a. letters in a foreign language
   b. pictures and shapes
   c. sentences and paragraphs
   d. music notes

- 68 -

43. How does Leopold feel after Wolfgang plays the beginning of the concerto?

    a. Amazed

    b. Amused

    c. Eager

    d. Awkward

44. What word in paragraph 4 best defines the word *intently*?

    a. Begged

    b. Laughed

    c. Serious

    d. Looking

45. What does the passage imply is the main reason for Wolfgang's musical skill?

    a. Talent

    b. Hard work

    c. His father's determination

    d. Hours of lessons

46. Based on the context of the passage, what is the meaning of the word *prodigy* as it is used in paragraph 3?

    a. Baby

    b. Genius

    c. Student

    d. Son

47. What is the most logical reason why Leopold wants Anna and Wolfgang to play the harpsichord?

    a. He wants his children to work hard

    b. He's also a musician

    c. He wants to impress his friends

    d. He knows Anna and Wolfgang love music and wants to please them

48. Look at the timeline below.

What event best fits in the missing arrow?

    a. Wolfgang plays a perfect chord on the harpsichord

    b. Wolfgang watches Anna's music lessons

    c. Wolfgang amazes Leopold's friend

    d. Wolfgang learns to play minuets in just a half hour

Answer Key and Explanations for Reading Test #2

TEKS Standard §110.20(b)(6)

1. B: The correct answer is B because the crab says in paragraph 24, "If this fellow once got hold of fish, he would never let them go in a pond." This sentence shows that the crab knows that he cannot trust the crane. Even though the crab says in paragraph 22 that he's worried he'll fall, he needs to defend himself from the crane because he's worried the crane will eat him. Choice C is incorrect because the crab is not friends with the crane; in fact, he does not trust the crane and is worried the crane will attack him. Although the crab is glad to leave the dry pond for the wet pond, he's worried about being transported on the crane because he knows that the crane will probably try to eat him.

TEKS Standard §110.20(b)(6)

2. C: In paragraph 11, the fish say that they think the crane is hoping to eat them, one after the other. They know that cranes like to eat fish and don't want to get eaten. Choice A is incorrect because skeptical means to not trust someone. If the crane liked helping the fish out, the fish would not be skeptical of him. Choice B is incorrect because the crane is not making the water run dry. Instead, paragraph 2 says that the water used to run short at the dry season. Choice D is incorrect because it is the crab that is worried he will fall, not the fish.

TEKS Standard §110.20(b)(2)(B)

3. A: The correct answer is choice A because paragraph 13 says that the fish was blind in one eye. Choice B is incorrect because the fish is blind in one eye, not two. While the passage does say that the fish is old, choice C is incorrect because the word *purblind* contains the root word *blind* and is probably related to not being able to see. While the other fish do trust the purblind fish, purblind is most likely related to the word *blind*.

TEKS Standard §110.20(b)(6)(A)

4. D: Choice D is the correct answer because the crab threatens to cut the crane's head off in paragraph 30. Choice A is incorrect because the crane demonstrates several times in the story that he does not keep his word. Choice B is incorrect because the crane intends to eat the crab instead of taking him to the pond. He only agrees to take the crab when he is threatened and does not care if the crab asks him. Choice C is incorrect because the Genius is a passive character that observes the crane's actions but does not interfere by giving him directions.

TEKS Standard §110.20(b)(6)

5. C: The correct answer is C because the author tells the story of the crane's trickery and then ends with a moral in verse. While the author does introduce Bodisat at the beginning of the story, Choice A is incorrect because Bodisat does not have a role in the crane's story; he only observes. Choice B is incorrect because the pond running dry is not the reason why the fish were eaten; the crane's trickery is the cause. Choice D is incorrect because the moral is at the end of the story, not the beginning.

TEKS Standard §110.20(b)(6)(A)

6. D: While all of the answer choices contain correct parts of the story, only choice D is fully correct. Choice A is incorrect because the crane does not drop the fish off at the pond; he eats them instead.

Choice B is incorrect because the crane does not take the crab straight to the pond. He tries to veer off to the tree to eat the crab and only goes to the pond when the crab threatens him. Choice C is incorrect because the crane does not eat the crab.

TEKS Standard §110.20(b)(6)

7. C: The correct answer is C because the mythical character of Bodisat and the moral at the end of the story show that the story is a fable. Choice A is incorrect because Bodisat is only mentioned at the beginning and end of the story; Bodisat observes the events but does not participate in them. Choice B is incorrect because the story does not display characteristics of non-fiction. For example, the animals speak, which cannot happen in a true story. Choice D is incorrect because realistic fiction portrays a made-up story that could happen in real life; since animals cannot talk in real life, the story cannot be realistic fiction.

TEKS Standard §110.20(b)(6)

8. C: The correct answer is C because the crane says in paragraph 3 that he wants to outwit the fish. Paragraph 5 says that the crane sat by the water and thought about how he should outwit the fish. Choice A is incorrect even though the crane pretends that he's worried about the fish. He pretends to worry about the fish so that he can convince them to go to the other pond. Therefore, he is lying in paragraph 8. Choice B is incorrect because the crane has not even met the crab in paragraph 6. Choice D is incorrect because the crane is lying in paragraph 10 when he talks about the large pond. He's really thinking about how he can trick the fish and find a way to eat them.

TEKS Standard §110.20(b)(6) and (6)(B)

9. C: Choice C is the correct answer because both the crane and crab are deceitful, or tricky. The crane is deceitful when he tricks the fish and convinces them to let him take them to the pond. The crab is deceitful when he plans to attack the crane if the crane does not take him to the pond. Choice A is incorrect because only the crab lives in the water. The story does not say where the crane lives. Choice B is incorrect because the story does not say that the crab eats fish; in fact, the story doesn't say what the crab eats at all. Choice D is incorrect because the crane and crab are not friends. The crane wants to eat the crab.

TEKS Standard §110.20(b)(6)

10. B: The correct answer is B because the crane points out the fish bones underneath the Varana tree. Choice A is incorrect because the crane does not show proof that the pond is larger in paragraph 30; he shows the crab the pond in paragraph 27. Choice C is incorrect because the crane is talking to the crab in 27; he hasn't eaten the crab and can't show proof. Choice D is incorrect because the crab, not the crane, says that the fish are stupid.

TEKS Standard §110.20(b)(6)(B)

11. B: The verse at the end of the story presents the moral and says villains won't prosper, or succeed, through villainy. Instead, villains win through deceit, or trickery. Choices A and D are incorrect because the moral says that villains don't succeed through villainy or evil. Choice C is incorrect because the moral does not say that clever villains are also evil. Instead, it says that the villain is clever.

TEKS Standard §110.20(b)(2)(B)

12. A: The correct answer is A because the second sentence of paragraph 26 says that the crab caught hold of his neck securely, which also means tightly. Choice B is incorrect because no adjectives in the paragraph show that the claws are sharp; instead, the claws are tight and very secure. While the crab does have plans to hurt the crane, choice C is incorrect because the phrase "blacksmith's pincers" simply shows how tightly and securely the crab is holding onto the crane. Choice D is incorrect because the shape of his claws does not show the crab's emotions; his claws do not change shape based on how he's feeling.

TEKS Standard §110.20(b)(6)

13. C: The correct answer is C because paragraph 7 says that the children consider the house to be like a Fairy Palace even though it "was not a pretty house at all". The children are wise because they are glad to be living in the country, since London was "like prison for children". Choice A is incorrect because the paragraph makes clear that the house is run down and not pretty. Despite its looks, the children still love the house. Although the house is less nice than it appeared at first glance, choice B is incorrect because the sentence "But the children were wiser for once" means that the children knew that they would love the house despite its run-down appearance. Choice D is incorrect because the children do not want to go back to London. They are excited to be living in the country and considered London to be like a prison.

TEKS Standard §110.20(b)(6)

14. C: Choice C is the correct answer because the sentence shows the eagerness the children felt when they arrived. There was a scramble to get out of the carriage because the children were so excited to explore the new house. Choice A is incorrect because the sentence simply describes the house and doesn't hint at emotions. Choice B is incorrect because it only show's Robert's awe that the house is so white; it doesn't show how all the children feel. Choice D is incorrect because the children were excited to explore even though the house wasn't pretty; this choice doesn't show the children's excitement or other emotions.

TEKS Standard §110.20(b)(6)

15. B: The correct answer is B because the new house is in the country and paragraph 7 says that the children had been in London for two years. Choice A is incorrect because it is the opposite of what happened in the story. Instead of moving to London, the children are moving to the country. Choice C is incorrect because the children are not moving to a new country; they are moving to the country, which is an area that is not near a city. Choice D is incorrect because the passage uses *prison* and *fairy palace* as metaphors. The children aren't moving from a literal prison to a real fairy palace. Instead, they're moving from a city that felt like a prison to a house that feels like a fairy palace.

TEKS Standard §110.20(b)(6)

16. A: The correct answer is choice A because Mother does not seem happy to move into the house. She does not join in the "glorious rush" and thinks that the house is "rather inconvenient". Choice B is incorrect because Mother's hesitation to see the new house shows that she's not excited. While it's true that mother does not seem to want to explore with the children, choice C is not as logical a reason as choice A. The main reason why Mother doesn't want to explore the house is because she is reluctant to move in. Choice D is incorrect because the passage does not indicate that the driver needs help. Instead, Mother watches him carry the boxes in and pays him. She does this instead of exploring because she is not excited to move in.

TEKS Standard §110.20(b)(6)

17. C: The correct answer is choice C because the passage does not say that the walk was long. The passage does say in paragraph 6 that the family had to open and pass through a long gate, but it does not say that it was a long walk. All of the other answer choices are supported by the passage. The first sentence of paragraph five says the walk was muddy and dark. Paragraph 5 also says there were no gas lamps on the road. The second sentence of paragraph five says that the road was rough, which means it was not smooth.

TEKS Standard §110.20(b)(6)

18. B: Choice B is the correct answer because the cart driver says that the train was late in paragraph 17. Choice A is incorrect; the cart driver says in paragraph 16 that Mrs. Viney has gone home, not that she's run an errand. Choice C is incorrect because Mrs. Viney wasn't in the house. Choice D is incorrect because the door was locked; the cart man fetched the key from under the doorstep in order to unlock it.

TEKS Standard §110.20(b)(6)

19. B: The correct answer is B because the details about the house show that it's neither homey nor cozy. For example, paragraph 24 says that there is a stone floor, no curtains, no hearth rug, no fire, and rats in the walls. Choice A is incorrect because the house is the opposite of homey and cozy. Choice C is incorrect because Mrs. Viney did not light a fire for the family; paragraph 24 says that the fireplace had "cold, dead ashes". Choice D is incorrect because there is furniture in the house. Paragraph 24 describes the kitchen table and chairs.

TEKS Standard §110.20(b)(6)

20. D: The correct answer is choice D because the cart man shows them the way to the house and is the only one who knows where the key is. The reader also knows that the children haven't been in this town before because paragraph 3 says that the train was the very first one they saw on the railway tracks. Choice A is incorrect because the children don't show excitement. They are tired and cold. Peter's observation that the garden looks like "dripping-pan full of black cabbages" shows that he and his siblings are not enchanted by the house. Choice B is incorrect because paragraph 3 makes it clear that the children will learn to love the railway but don't love it yet. Choice C is incorrect because paragraphs 8 and 9 make it clear that the family does not know Mrs. Viney. Roberta asks who Mrs. Viney is and Mother explains that she hired Mrs. Viney to clean the house.

TEKS Standard §110.20(b)(6)

21. D: The best answer is choice D because the surrounding context shows that the phrase is talking about the railway. Since the story is called "The Railway Children", it is logical that the children might get this name because they love the railway. Although the other choices mention the train, they don't illustrate the reason why the author chose the title "The Railway Children" because they don't show the children's feelings about the railway. Choice A simply describes the action of removing the baggage from the train, choice B describes the train's engine, and choice C describes the children watching the train chug away.

TEKS Standard §110.20(b)(6)

22. B: The correct answer is choice B because both children are moving to a new house that they don't seem to know anything about. Choices A and C are incorrect because only the children in "Five Children and It" are excited when they see the house, and only the children in "The Railway Children" are disappointed. "Five Children and It" hints that the children are eager to explore the country in addition to the house, but choice D is also incorrect because the children in "The Railway Children" do not show this eagerness.

TEKS Standard §110.20(b)(6)

23. C: Choice C is the best answer because Mother in "Five Children and It" is not eager to see the new house and is not excited to move. Likewise, Mother in "The Railway Children" is also unhappy, as shown in paragraph 23 when she speaks "rather less cheerfully than usual". Choice A is incorrect because it states a fact rather than showing Mother's emotion. Choice B is incorrect because the words "Here we are" do not show Mother's state of mind; from these words, the reader cannot determine if mother is disappointed or excited to be at the house. Choice D is incorrect because it describes the house's location but doesn't show Mother's feelings.

TEKS Standard §110.20(b)(6)

24. D: Paragraph 7 in "Five Children and It" show that the children are very excited to explore their new house and are looking forward to living in the country. Many details from "The Railway Children" show that the children in that story are not excited about moving or their new house. For example, paragraph 2 says that they were melancholy and paragraph 12 describes the garden as a pan of black cabbages. Choices A and B are incorrect because the children in "Five Children and It" thought that living in London was like being in a prison; they don't feel the same way about their new house. Choice A is also incorrect because the children in "The Railway Children" are not excited to explore their new house; they seem reluctant to move. Choice C is incorrect because it's the children in "Five Children and It" that think the new house is wonderful. Likewise, the children in "The Railway Children" are the ones who are disappointed.

TEKS Standard §110.20(b)(6)

25. A: The correct answer is choice A because both families are moving to a new home in a new area, or setting. Choice B is incorrect because the children in "Five Children and It" don't seem uncomfortable; instead, they are very eager. Choice C is incorrect because the passages describe the houses in detail but don't focus on the characters. Although the children in "Five Children and It" don't feel the same way as Mother about the new house, nothing in the passages foreshadows an argument with the parents. The children seem to respect and get along with their mothers.

TEKS Standard §110.20(b)(9)

26. D: The correct answer is D because the author says in paragraph 7 that the ancient Britons were divided into many tribes, each of which had its own king. The author implies that these tribes fought among each other. While paragraph 7 also says the ancient Britons had many weapons, it doesn't say that the weapons were the reason that they fought. Instead, it simply says that they fought with the weapons. Choice B is incorrect because paragraph 7 says that the ancient Britons constantly fought. However, the passage stops discussing the Phoenicians after paragraph 4. Choice C is incorrect because paragraph 6 says that there were no roads or bridges. The author gives this detail in order to describe the land. This detail does not support paragraph 7, which says the ancient Britons frequently fought.

- 74 -

TEKS Standard §110.20(b)(9)

27. B: The correct answer is B because paragraph 2 describes the natural details of the islands. For example, the paragraph describes the foaming waves, the cliffs, and the winds that blew over the forests. Choice A is incorrect because the map is discussed in paragraph 1, not paragraph 2. Choice C is incorrect because paragraph 2 only briefly mentions the people who lived on the islands. The author uses paragraphs 3-5 to give more details about the people who lived on the islands. Choice D is incorrect because the answer choice is only a portion of paragraph 2. The paragraph describes many natural features of the islands in addition to the winds and waves.

TEKS Standard §110.20(b)(9)

28. D: The correct answer is D because the word 'grew' shows that the ancient Britons changed after the Phoenicians arrived. Choice A is incorrect because the answer choice only shows something that the Phoenicians did with the Britons; however, it does not describe how the Britons changed. Choice B is incorrect because the sentence only talks about the Phoenicians and does not mention the ancient Britons. Choice C is incorrect because it refers to the French and Belgians who moved to the England; it does not mention the ancient Britons.

TEKS Standard §110.20(b)(9)

29. B: The author describes the history of the islands and gives informative details about the islands and the people who lived there in the past. Choice A is incorrect because the author does not make jokes during the article; instead, he simply describes facts. Choice C is incorrect because the author does not display anger or any other emotions; he simply describes facts. Choice D is incorrect because the author proves that he's very interested in the topic by giving many descriptive details. Therefore, he is the opposite of bored.

TEKS Standard §110.20(b)(8)

30. B: The word *solitary* refers to isolation, or being alone. Furthermore, the sentence says that the islands are alone in a great expanse of water, which shows that other lands do not surround the islands. Choice A is incorrect because the sentence only talks about the size of the small islands off Scotland. It does not talk about where the islands are in relation to other, bigger lands. Choice C is incorrect because it shows the islanders' relationship with the sea. However, it does not talk about the separation that the islanders have with other people. Choice D is incorrect because it shows the opposite of isolation; the sentence shows how the people who came to the islands (such as the French, Belgians, and Spanish) mixed with the ancient Britons.

TEKS Standard §110.20(b)(9)

31. A: The correct answer is choice A because paragraph 1 acts as an introductory passage. It starts by describing the islands on the map. Paragraph 2 moves into the earliest history of the islands. Later paragraphs describe the history as more and more groups of people came to them. Because of this organization, the passage best fits at the beginning of a longer work. The reader can infer that the author will continue describing the history of Britain throughout the rest of the work. Choices B, C, and D are incorrect because the first paragraphs of the passage are introductory.

TEKS Standard §110.20(b)(9)

32. B: The correct answer is B because the first part of the sentence describes the boats that the ancient Britons built. However, the phrase "But seldom, if ever, ventured far from the shore" says that the boats didn't go far from shore. This implies that the boats may not have been used much. Choice A is incorrect because the phrase does not talk about specific ways that the ancient Britons used the boats. Even though the author describes weapons in the same paragraph, the phrase in the question focuses on the boats that the people made. The paragraph only moves onto weapons in the second sentence. Choice D is incorrect because the author does not connect the boats (discussed in paragraph 7) to the fortresses (discussed in at the end of paragraph 6).

TEKS Standard §110.20(b)(9)

33. C: Choice C is the best answer because paragraph 4 says that the tin and lead tempted some French and Belgian people to come over. Choice A is incorrect because 'white cliffs' are only mentioned by the Phoenicians when they are trying to explain to the French and Belgians where they have found the tin and lead. They point across the sea to the islands, using the white cliffs as a landmark. Choice B is incorrect because the fine weather was only mentioned as an example of when it is possible to see the cliffs. However, the weather was not mentioned as a way of convincing the French and Belgians to come over to the islands. Choice D is incorrect because the juices of plants were used by the islanders to paint their bodies.

TEKS Standard §110.20(b)(9)

34. C: The correct answer is C because the passage is informational and intended to teach children about the history of Britain. Choice A is incorrect because a newspaper is used to discuss current events and does not typically have long articles about history. While travel books sometimes have historical information, choice B is incorrect because the passage only talks about history. It does not describe the sites that travelers could expect to see. Choice D is incorrect because a novel is fictional, and this passage is non-fiction, or true.

TEKS Standard §110.20(b)(9)

35. D: The correct answer is choice D, as shown by paragraphs 3 and 4. The first sentence of paragraph 3 says that the Phoenicians found tin and lead on the islands. The first sentence of paragraph 4 says that the Phoenicians traded with the Islanders, who were also called the ancient Britons. Finally, the second-to-last sentence of paragraph 4 says that the French and Belgians settled in England. Choices A, B, and C are incorrect because they do not show the correct order that is described above.

TEKS Standard §110.20(b)(9)

36. A: Choice A is the best answer because paragraph 1 describes the location of the islands on the map. Readers know that they can find the islands by looking in the left-hand upper corner of the Eastern Hemisphere. Choice B is incorrect because paragraph six says that there were no roads that ran through England, Scotland, or Ireland during the time period that the passage is describing. Choice C is incorrect because the details about the small islands are only a small portion of the first paragraph. Most of the paragraph describes how the islands appear on the map. Choice D is incorrect because the paragraph does not mention the size of the main islands. Furthermore, the paragraph does not mention France or Belgium; these countries are first mentioned in paragraph 4.

TEKS Standard §110.20(b)(9)

37. C: Choice C is the correct answer because this answer choice describes the lands by mentioning swamps and forests. Choice A is incorrect because it does not give details of the lands and also does not mention the interior of the islands, which is first mentioned in paragraph 5. While choice B

- 76 -

mentions the interior, it is incorrect because it only says that it is away from the sea. It does not give details about the lands. Choice D is incorrect because it discusses the dynamics of the tribes and the relationships between the people rather than the features of the lands, such as the swamps and forests.

TEKS Standard §110.20(b)(6)

38. C: The best answer is choice C because Leopold calls Wolfgang a baby in paragraph 5. He then tells Wolfgang to wait awhile, meaning that he will teach Wolfgang harpsichord when he is older. Choice A is incorrect because Leopold does not yet know that Wolfgang is talented. He only discovers that Wolfgang is talented after he plays the perfect chord in paragraph 5. Choice B is incorrect because Wolfgang first shows his talent in paragraph 5. Leopold does not realize that Wolfgang is a musical genius until paragraph 7, which is after Wolfgang has been taking lessons for some time. Choice D is incorrect because Leopold clearly implies in paragraph 5 that he plans on teaching Wolfgang harpsichord when he is older.

TEKS Standard §110.20(b)(9)

39. B: While it's possible that someone recorded the exact dialogue between Wolfgang and Leopold, it is more likely that the author invented it in order to tell a story. Since this scene took place in front of few witnesses who could remember the words and because there are no recording devices, it's unlikely that the exact words of the dialogue are true. Choice A is incorrect because the author should have been able to find the exact names of Wolfgang and his family members through historical research. Choice C is incorrect because it's logical that Wolfgang and his father might remember the exact age that Wolfgang wrote a concerto, which would be considered a huge accomplishment worth remembering. It is more likely that the dialogue is made up because the many words of dialogue would be more difficult to remember than Wolfgang's age. Choice D is incorrect because Leopold likely remembered how quickly Wolfgang learned due to his being very proud of him.

TEKS Standard §110.20(b)(6)

40. C: The correct answer is C because the sentence gives Anna's name and then gives her nickname, Nannerl, in parentheses. The nickname Nannerl is in the same form as Wolferl (-erl at the end). This detail helps the reader understand that Wolferl is Wolfgang's nickname. Choice A is incorrect because the sentence simply gives five of Wolfgang's names. Although one of the names is Wolfgangus, the reader doesn't yet know that Wolfgang's father is likely to abbreviate Wolfgang with the –erl ending. Although choice B also includes Wolfgang's name, it is incorrect because it does not show the types of nicknames used in Wolfgang's time. Choice D is incorrect because it does not give Wolfgang's name or explain how it is shortened into a nickname.

TEKS Standard §110.20(b)(6)

41. C: The correct answer is C because paragraph 5 shows that Wolfgang plays a chord by himself. The author emphasizes this feat by italicizing the words "perfect chord". Choice A is incorrect because Anna does not speak or ask anything at any point in the passage. Choice B is incorrect because Wolfgang does not *ask* his father to learn harpsichord. Instead, he comes into the lesson and shows his father that he wants to learn harpsichord by giving him a serious look (paragraph 4). Choice D is incorrect because Wolfgang composes the concerto in paragraphs 8-17, which is after he has already started taking harpsichord lessons.

TEKS Standard §110.20(b)(8)

42. D: Although hieroglyphics typically refers to letters in ancient Egyptian, they refer to music notes in this passage. It is clear that the 'hieroglyphics' refer to music notes in paragraph 11 when Wolfgang says that he is composing a concerto for the harpsichord. Choice A is incorrect because the word 'hieroglyphics' in paragraph 8 does not refer to the usual definition. While hieroglyphics are often made up of pictures and shapes, choice B is incorrect because they refer to the music notes used to compose the concerto. Choice C is incorrect because Wolfgang is composing or writing a concerto, not an essay.

TEKS Standard §110.20(b)(6)

43. A: The correct answer is choice A because paragraph 17 says "now looked at each other with wonder not untouched with awe." The words *wonder* and *awe* are synonymous with *amazed*. Although the passage says that Leopold and his friend exchanged amused glances (paragraphs 14 and 17), choice B is incorrect because they did not stay amused once they heard the concerto. Choice C is incorrect because Leopold was eager before he heard the concerto. Paragraph 14 says that he eagerly picked up Wolfgang's concerto to look at the music notes. Choice D is incorrect because the passage does not say that Leopold felt awkward or uncomfortable. Although paragraph 17 uses the similar-sounding word *awe*, this means wonder or amazement, not awkwardness.

TEKS Standard §110.20(b)(2)(B)

44. C: The correct answer is C because the paragraph says "glancing down into the child's serious face". This phrase defines the word *intently* as *serious*. While it's true that Wolfgang begs his father for harpsichord lessons, the word *intently* refers to the serious look on Wolfgang's face and not the words he used when he asked for harpsichord lessons. Choice B is incorrect because *intently* refers to the look on Wolfgang's face, but the paragraph says that Leopold laughed. Therefore, Leopold was amused, not Wolfgang. Choice D is incorrect because *looking* is a verb that indicates what Wolfgang is doing. The word *intently* is an adverb that modifies the verb and shows how Wolfgang was looking at his father.

TEKS Standard §110.20(b)(6)

45. A: Although all the answer choices contributed to Wolfgang's abilities the best answer is choice A because the passage shows that his talent was the main reason for his success. The passage says several times that Wolfgang was a musical genius, or very talented, and that he had a lot of musical ability. Other parts of the passage, such as paragraph 7, show that Wolfgang was able to play the harpsichord without much work at a very young age. Choices B, C, and D are incorrect because these three options supplemented Wolfgang's extraordinary talent but were not the main reason for his skill with music.

TEKS Standard §110.20(b)(2)(B)

46. B: Although paragraph 3 does not use the word *genius*, the passage frequently refers to Wolfgang as a musical genius. For example, paragraph 2 calls him a "great genius". Choice A is incorrect because the word *prodigy* refers to Wolfgang's skill rather than his age. The paragraph talks about the things he was doing despite his age; these feats made him a prodigy, or genius. Choice C is incorrect because Wolfgang is not yet a music student. In fact, he would like to be a music student, but his father says in paragraph 5 that Wolfgang is too young for music lessons. Choice D is incorrect because the word *prodigy* does not refer to Wolfgang's relationship to his father. The adjective *musical* indicates that *prodigy* refers to Wolfgang's music ability.

TEKS Standard §110.20(b)(6)

47. B: Choice B is the best answer because the paragraph 7 says that Leopold was a talented musician. It also says that he was very proud that both of his children had musical talent. Although Leopold may have given Anna and Wolfgang a lot of work during music lessons, choice A is incorrect because it's not the most logical reason Leopold taught his children the harpsichord. If he simply wanted them to work hard, he could have engaged them in other activities. Choice C is incorrect because it is more logical that Leopold wants his children to excel in something that he also enjoys. Being able to impress his friends is an added bonus but not Leopold's main reason in teaching his children to play the harpsichord. Choice D is incorrect because nothing in the passage indicates that Leopold wants to please his children. Instead, paragraph 7 refers to Leopold's own musical abilities.

TEKS Standard §110.20(b)(6)

48. D: The passage describes Wolfgang's lessons in paragraph 6 and introduces the concerto in paragraph 8. The paragraph in between, paragraph 7, says that Wolfgang was able to learn minuets in under a half hour. Choice A is incorrect because Wolfgang played a perfect chord on the harpsichord the very first time he played the harpsichord, which happens in the first arrow. Choice B is incorrect because Wolfgang watches Anna's music lessons in paragraph 3, before he plays the harpsichord for the first time. Choice C is incorrect because Wolfgang amazes Leopold's friend in paragraph 17, after he writes the concerto.

How to Overcome Test Anxiety

Just the thought of taking a test is enough to make most people a little nervous. A test is an important event that can have a long-term impact on your future, so it's important to take it seriously and it's natural to feel anxious about performing well. But just because anxiety is normal, that doesn't mean that it's helpful in test taking, or that you should simply accept it as part of your life. Anxiety can have a variety of effects. These effects can be mild, like making you feel slightly nervous, or severe, like blocking your ability to focus or remember even a simple detail.

If you experience test anxiety—whether severe or mild—it's important to know how to beat it. To discover this, first you need to understand what causes test anxiety.

Causes of Test Anxiety

While we often think of anxiety as an uncontrollable emotional state, it can actually be caused by simple, practical things. One of the most common causes of test anxiety is that a person does not feel adequately prepared for their test. This feeling can be the result of many different issues such as poor study habits or lack of organization, but the most common culprit is time management. Starting to study too late, failing to organize your study time to cover all of the material, or being distracted while you study will mean that you're not well prepared for the test. This may lead to cramming the night before, which will cause you to be physically and mentally exhausted for the test. Poor time management also contributes to feelings of stress, fear, and hopelessness as you realize you are not well prepared but don't know what to do about it.

Other times, test anxiety is not related to your preparation for the test but comes from unresolved fear. This may be a past failure on a test, or poor performance on tests in general. It may come from comparing yourself to others who seem to be performing better or from the stress of living up to expectations. Anxiety may be driven by fears of the future—how failure on this test would affect your educational and career goals. These fears are often completely irrational, but they can still negatively impact your test performance.

> **Review Video:** 3 Reasons You Have Test Anxiety
> Visit mometrix.com/academy and enter code: 428468

Elements of Test Anxiety

As mentioned earlier, test anxiety is considered to be an emotional state, but it has physical and mental components as well. Sometimes you may not even realize that you are suffering from test anxiety until you notice the physical symptoms. These can include trembling hands, rapid heartbeat, sweating, nausea, and tense muscles. Extreme anxiety may lead to fainting or vomiting. Obviously, any of these symptoms can have a negative impact on testing. It is important to recognize them as soon as they begin to occur so that you can address the problem before it damages your performance.

> **Review Video:** 3 Ways to Tell You Have Test Anxiety
> Visit mometrix.com/academy and enter code: 927847

The mental components of test anxiety include trouble focusing and inability to remember learned information. During a test, your mind is on high alert, which can help you recall information and stay focused for an extended period of time. However, anxiety interferes with your mind's natural processes, causing you to blank out, even on the questions you know well. The strain of testing during anxiety makes it difficult to stay focused, especially on a test that may take several hours. Extreme anxiety can take a huge mental toll, making it difficult not only to recall test information but even to understand the test questions or pull your thoughts together.

> **Review Video:** How Test Anxiety Affects Memory
> Visit mometrix.com/academy and enter code: 609003

Effects of Test Anxiety

Test anxiety is like a disease—if left untreated, it will get progressively worse. Anxiety leads to poor performance, and this reinforces the feelings of fear and failure, which in turn lead to poor performances on subsequent tests. It can grow from a mild nervousness to a crippling condition. If allowed to progress, test anxiety can have a big impact on your schooling, and consequently on your future.

Test anxiety can spread to other parts of your life. Anxiety on tests can become anxiety in any stressful situation, and blanking on a test can turn into panicking in a job situation. But fortunately, you don't have to let anxiety rule your testing and determine your grades. There are a number of relatively simple steps you can take to move past anxiety and function normally on a test and in the rest of life.

> **Review Video:** How Test Anxiety Impacts Your Grades
> Visit mometrix.com/academy and enter code: 939819

Physical Steps for Beating Test Anxiety

While test anxiety is a serious problem, the good news is that it can be overcome. It doesn't have to control your ability to think and remember information. While it may take time, you can begin taking steps today to beat anxiety.

Just as your first hint that you may be struggling with anxiety comes from the physical symptoms, the first step to treating it is also physical. Rest is crucial for having a clear, strong mind. If you are tired, it is much easier to give in to anxiety. But if you establish good sleep habits, your body and mind will be ready to perform optimally, without the strain of exhaustion. Additionally, sleeping well helps you to retain information better, so you're more likely to recall the answers when you see the test questions.

Getting good sleep means more than going to bed on time. It's important to allow your brain time to relax. Take study breaks from time to time so it doesn't get overworked, and don't study right before bed. Take time to rest your mind before trying to rest your body, or you may find it difficult to fall asleep.

> **Review Video: <u>The Importance of Sleep for Your Brain</u>**
> Visit mometrix.com/academy and enter code: 319338

Along with sleep, other aspects of physical health are important in preparing for a test. Good nutrition is vital for good brain function. Sugary foods and drinks may give a burst of energy but this burst is followed by a crash, both physically and emotionally. Instead, fuel your body with protein and vitamin-rich foods.

Also, drink plenty of water. Dehydration can lead to headaches and exhaustion, especially if your brain is already under stress from the rigors of the test. Particularly if your test is a long one, drink water during the breaks. And if possible, take an energy-boosting snack to eat between sections.

> **Review Video: <u>How Diet Can Affect your Mood</u>**
> Visit mometrix.com/academy and enter code: 624317

Along with sleep and diet, a third important part of physical health is exercise. Maintaining a steady workout schedule is helpful, but even taking 5-minute study breaks to walk can help get your blood pumping faster and clear your head. Exercise also releases endorphins, which contribute to a positive feeling and can help combat test anxiety.

When you nurture your physical health, you are also contributing to your mental health. If your body is healthy, your mind is much more likely to be healthy as well. So take time to rest, nourish your body with healthy food and water, and get moving as much as possible. Taking these physical steps will make you stronger and more able to take the mental steps necessary to overcome test anxiety.

> **Review Video: <u>How to Stay Healthy and Prevent Test Anxiety</u>**
> Visit mometrix.com/academy and enter code: 877894

Mental Steps for Beating Test Anxiety

Working on the mental side of test anxiety can be more challenging, but as with the physical side, there are clear steps you can take to overcome it. As mentioned earlier, test anxiety often stems from lack of preparation, so the obvious solution is to prepare for the test. Effective studying may be the most important weapon you have for beating test anxiety, but you can and should employ several other mental tools to combat fear.

First, boost your confidence by reminding yourself of past success—tests or projects that you aced. If you're putting as much effort into preparing for this test as you did for those, there's no reason you should expect to fail here. Work hard to prepare; then trust your preparation.

Second, surround yourself with encouraging people. It can be helpful to find a study group, but be sure that the people you're around will encourage a positive attitude. If you spend time with others who are anxious or cynical, this will only contribute to your own anxiety. Look for others who are motivated to study hard from a desire to succeed, not from a fear of failure.

Third, reward yourself. A test is physically and mentally tiring, even without anxiety, and it can be helpful to have something to look forward to. Plan an activity following the test, regardless of the outcome, such as going to a movie or getting ice cream.

When you are taking the test, if you find yourself beginning to feel anxious, remind yourself that you know the material. Visualize successfully completing the test. Then take a few deep, relaxing breaths and return to it. Work through the questions carefully but with confidence, knowing that you are capable of succeeding.

Developing a healthy mental approach to test taking will also aid in other areas of life. Test anxiety affects more than just the actual test—it can be damaging to your mental health and even contribute to depression. It's important to beat test anxiety before it becomes a problem for more than testing.

> **Review Video: Test Anxiety and Depression**
> Visit mometrix.com/academy and enter code: 904704

Study Strategy

Being prepared for the test is necessary to combat anxiety, but what does being prepared look like? You may study for hours on end and still not feel prepared. What you need is a strategy for test prep. The next few pages outline our recommended steps to help you plan out and conquer the challenge of preparation.

Step 1: Scope Out the Test

Learn everything you can about the format (multiple choice, essay, etc.) and what will be on the test. Gather any study materials, course outlines, or sample exams that may be available. Not only will this help you to prepare, but knowing what to expect can help to alleviate test anxiety.

Step 2: Map Out the Material

Look through the textbook or study guide and make note of how many chapters or sections it has. Then divide these over the time you have. For example, if a book has 15 chapters and you have five days to study, you need to cover three chapters each day. Even better, if you have the time, leave an extra day at the end for overall review after you have gone through the material in depth.

If time is limited, you may need to prioritize the material. Look through it and make note of which sections you think you already have a good grasp on, and which need review. While you are studying, skim quickly through the familiar sections and take more time on the challenging parts. Write out your plan so you don't get lost as you go. Having a written plan also helps you feel more in control of the study, so anxiety is less likely to arise from feeling overwhelmed at the amount to cover. A sample plan may look like this:

- Day 1: Skim chapters 1–4, study chapter 5 (especially pages 31–33)
- Day 2: Study chapters 6–7, skim chapters 8–9
- Day 3: Skim chapter 10, study chapters 11–12 (especially pages 87–90)
- Day 4: Study chapters 13–15
- Day 5: Overall review (focus most on chapters 5, 6, and 12), take practice test

Step 3: Gather Your Tools

Decide what study method works best for you. Do you prefer to highlight in the book as you study and then go back over the highlighted portions? Or do you type out notes of the important information? Or is it helpful to make flashcards that you can carry with you? Assemble the pens, index cards, highlighters, post-it notes, and any other materials you may need so you won't be distracted by getting up to find things while you study.

If you're having a hard time retaining the information or organizing your notes, experiment with different methods. For example, try color-coding by subject with colored pens, highlighters, or post-it notes. If you learn better by hearing, try recording yourself reading your notes so you can listen while in the car, working out, or simply sitting at your desk. Ask a friend to quiz you from your flashcards, or try teaching someone the material to solidify it in your mind.

Step 4: Create Your Environment

It's important to avoid distractions while you study. This includes both the obvious distractions like visitors and the subtle distractions like an uncomfortable chair (or a too-comfortable couch that makes you want to fall asleep). Set up the best study environment possible: good lighting and a comfortable work area. If background music helps you focus, you may want to turn it on, but otherwise keep the room quiet. If you are using a computer to take notes, be sure you don't have any other windows open, especially applications like social media, games, or anything else that could distract you. Silence your phone and turn off notifications. Be sure to keep water close by so you stay hydrated while you study (but avoid unhealthy drinks and snacks).

Also, take into account the best time of day to study. Are you freshest first thing in the morning? Try to set aside some time then to work through the material. Is your mind clearer in the afternoon or evening? Schedule your study session then. Another method is to study at the same time of day that you will take the test, so that your brain gets used to working on the material at that time and will be ready to focus at test time.

Step 5: Study!

Once you have done all the study preparation, it's time to settle into the actual studying. Sit down, take a few moments to settle your mind so you can focus, and begin to follow your study plan. Don't give in to distractions or let yourself procrastinate. This is your time to prepare so you'll be ready to fearlessly approach the test. Make the most of the time and stay focused.

Of course, you don't want to burn out. If you study too long you may find that you're not retaining the information very well. Take regular study breaks. For example, taking five minutes out of every hour to walk briskly, breathing deeply and swinging your arms, can help your mind stay fresh.

As you get to the end of each chapter or section, it's a good idea to do a quick review. Remind yourself of what you learned and work on any difficult parts. When you feel that you've mastered the material, move on to the next part. At the end of your study session, briefly skim through your notes again.

But while review is helpful, cramming last minute is NOT. If at all possible, work ahead so that you won't need to fit all your study into the last day. Cramming overloads your brain with more information than it can process and retain, and your tired mind may struggle to recall even previously learned information when it is overwhelmed with last-minute study. Also, the urgent nature of cramming and the stress placed on your brain contribute to anxiety. You'll be more likely to go to the test feeling unprepared and having trouble thinking clearly.

So don't cram, and don't stay up late before the test, even just to review your notes at a leisurely pace. Your brain needs rest more than it needs to go over the information again. In fact, plan to finish your studies by noon or early afternoon the day before the test. Give your brain the rest of the day to relax or focus on other things, and get a good night's sleep. Then you will be fresh for the test and better able to recall what you've studied.

Step 6: Take a practice test

Many courses offer sample tests, either online or in the study materials. This is an excellent resource to check whether you have mastered the material, as well as to prepare for the test format and environment.

Check the test format ahead of time: the number of questions, the type (multiple choice, free response, etc.), and the time limit. Then create a plan for working through them. For example, if you have 30 minutes to take a 60-question test, your limit is 30 seconds per question. Spend less time on the questions you know well so that you can take more time on the difficult ones.

If you have time to take several practice tests, take the first one open book, with no time limit. Work through the questions at your own pace and make sure you fully understand them. Gradually work up to taking a test under test conditions: sit at a desk with all study materials put away and set a timer. Pace yourself to make sure you finish the test with time to spare and go back to check your answers if you have time.

After each test, check your answers. On the questions you missed, be sure you understand why you missed them. Did you misread the question (tests can use tricky wording)? Did you forget the information? Or was it something you hadn't learned? Go back and study any shaky areas that the practice tests reveal.

Taking these tests not only helps with your grade, but also aids in combating test anxiety. If you're already used to the test conditions, you're less likely to worry about it, and working through tests until you're scoring well gives you a confidence boost. Go through the practice tests until you feel comfortable, and then you can go into the test knowing that you're ready for it.

Test Tips

On test day, you should be confident, knowing that you've prepared well and are ready to answer the questions. But aside from preparation, there are several test day strategies you can employ to maximize your performance.

First, as stated before, get a good night's sleep the night before the test (and for several nights before that, if possible). Go into the test with a fresh, alert mind rather than staying up late to study.

Try not to change too much about your normal routine on the day of the test. It's important to eat a nutritious breakfast, but if you normally don't eat breakfast at all, consider eating just a protein bar. If you're a coffee drinker, go ahead and have your normal coffee. Just make sure you time it so that the caffeine doesn't wear off right in the middle of your test. Avoid sugary beverages, and drink enough water to stay hydrated but not so much that you need a restroom break 10 minutes into the test. If your test isn't first thing in the morning, consider going for a walk or doing a light workout before the test to get your blood flowing.

Allow yourself enough time to get ready, and leave for the test with plenty of time to spare so you won't have the anxiety of scrambling to arrive in time. Another reason to be early is to select a good seat. It's helpful to sit away from doors and windows, which can be distracting. Find a good seat, get out your supplies, and settle your mind before the test begins.

When the test begins, start by going over the instructions carefully, even if you already know what to expect. Make sure you avoid any careless mistakes by following the directions.

Then begin working through the questions, pacing yourself as you've practiced. If you're not sure on an answer, don't spend too much time on it, and don't let it shake your confidence. Either skip it and come back later, or eliminate as many wrong answers as possible and guess among the remaining ones. Don't dwell on these questions as you continue—put them out of your mind and focus on what lies ahead.

Be sure to read all of the answer choices, even if you're sure the first one is the right answer. Sometimes you'll find a better one if you keep reading. But don't second-guess yourself if you do immediately know the answer. Your gut instinct is usually right. Don't let test anxiety rob you of the information you know.

If you have time at the end of the test (and if the test format allows), go back and review your answers. Be cautious about changing any, since your first instinct tends to be correct, but make sure you didn't misread any of the questions or accidentally mark the wrong answer choice. Look over any you skipped and make an educated guess.

At the end, leave the test feeling confident. You've done your best, so don't waste time worrying about your performance or wishing you could change anything. Instead, celebrate the successful completion of this test. And finally, use this test to learn how to deal with anxiety even better next time.

> **Review Video:** <u>5 Tips to Beat Test Anxiety</u>
> Visit mometrix.com/academy and enter code: 570656

Important Qualification

Not all anxiety is created equal. If your test anxiety is causing major issues in your life beyond the classroom or testing center, or if you are experiencing troubling physical symptoms related to your anxiety, it may be a sign of a serious physiological or psychological condition. If this sounds like your situation, we strongly encourage you to seek professional help.

Thank You

We at Mometrix would like to extend our heartfelt thanks to you, our friend and patron, for allowing us to play a part in your journey. It is a privilege to serve people from all walks of life who are unified in their commitment to building the best future they can for themselves.

The preparation you devote to these important testing milestones may be the most valuable educational opportunity you have for making a real difference in your life. We encourage you to put your heart into it—that feeling of succeeding, overcoming, and yes, conquering will be well worth the hours you've invested.

We want to hear your story, your struggles and your successes, and if you see any opportunities for us to improve our materials so we can help others even more effectively in the future, please share that with us as well. **The team at Mometrix would be absolutely thrilled to hear from you!** So please, send us an email (support@mometrix.com) and let's stay in touch.

If you'd like some additional help, check out these other resources we offer for your exam:

http://MometrixFlashcards.com/STAAR

Additional Bonus Material

Due to our efforts to try to keep this book to a manageable length, we've created a link that will give you access to all of your additional bonus material.

Please visit https://www.mometrix.com/bonus948/staarg8read to access the information.